Personal Liability in Public Service Organisations

A Legal Research Study for the Committee on Standards in Public Life

by Elizabeth Hambley of the Treasury Solicitor's Department

Standards in
Public Life

First published 1998

ISBN 0 11 430150 6

Contents

Introduction

In its examination of local spending bodies, the Committee on Standards in Public Life received evidence from witnesses and correspondents raising concerns about the personal legal liability of governors, board members and trustees of public institutions. In particular, there was a perception that the law lacked consistency in its treatment of those who serve voluntarily on bodies providing public services.

In recommendation 45 of its *Local Public Spending Bodies Report*, published in May 1996, the Committee concluded that:

> "The Government should seek to ensure broad consistency and adequate protection in respect of the personal liability of all appointed or elected members, directors, trustees and others responsible for bodies providing public services."

In its response published in January 1997, the then Government stated that:

> "... arrangements in this area need to be satisfactory, so as to avoid deterring those who would otherwise put themselves forward for public service on the basis of little or no financial reward."

The Committee and the Government agreed that a sensible first step towards achieving this aim would be to commission legal research into the problem. This study has been prepared accordingly.

Terms of reference

Its terms of reference are:

To undertake the necessary legal research to provide a report which:

- lists by legal status the various classes of public service organisation which fall within the scope of the study;

- sets out the present position in law regarding the personal legal liability of members of the governing bodies of these organisations;

- distinguishes between legal provisions common to all members, and those peculiar to particular classes or types of organisation;

- analyses the reasons for, and the significance of, legal differences between organisations;

- considers whether assessment can be made of the probability of particular risks arising; and

- undertakes a review of the range and scope of protective measures which are available to members of governing bodies.

The study is concerned with the law of England and Wales. The position in Scotland and Northern Ireland has not been examined. The study attempts to deal with the law as it stood in February 1998.

Every effort has been made to ensure that this study is both accurate and comprehensive in its analysis of the legal liability of individuals. However, the information contained in the study is, by its very nature, a general examination of the subject. Where readers have queries concerning a particular problem they should take appropriate legal advice. The Committee and the author regret that they cannot accept responsibility for any reliance which may be placed upon the contents of this study.

Recommendations

The Committee on Standards in Public Life has reached a number of conclusions based on the study. These are contained in a letter to the Prime Minister from Lord Neill of Bladen, chairman of the Committee, dated June 1998. A copy of the letter is being distributed with this study, or may be obtained from the Committee on Standards in Public Life, Horse Guards Road, London SW1P 3AL, telephone 0171 270 6455.

Scheme of the study

This is a legal study, setting out the circumstances in which people may find themselves personally liable for events associated with the public bodies on which they serve voluntarily.

It describes the various legal duties and responsibilities involved, and indicates how liability will vary for individuals, depending on the type of public body on which they serve.

The study concerns itself particularly with the theoretical application of current relevant law. But a wide range of real-life public service organisations (PSOs) has also been considered. These organisations are listed at Appendix A.

They fall into a number of different legal classes which provide the initial focus for the study, since they determine how personal liability may vary. The study is therefore set out as follows:

Summary

This offers a brief overview of the study and its conclusions.

Definitions

This section defines the main terms used in the study including 'public service organisation' (PSO), 'responsible body' and 'appointee'.

Chapter 1 – Public service organisations

This chapter describes the various types of PSO studied and introduces the legal classes into which they fall. It explains various assumptions made about the PSOs for the purpose of the study.

Chapter 2 – Appointees to PSOs

This chapter describes and defines the types of appointed or elected persons whose potential liability is at issue, and whose position is the principal consideration of the study.

Chapter 3 – The legal structures explained

This chapter explains the law which underpins each PSO and its responsible body. It draws attention, amongst other things, to the important legal distinctions between the organisation itself, its membership, and those responsible for its governance. It deals also with the vital issue of how charity law applies to public service organisations.

Chapter 4 – The solvent PSO: duties and responsibilities

This chapter sets out the legal duties and requirements laid upon appointees to PSOs, and discusses the potential legal liabilities that arise from them. It deals only with the situation in PSOs which remain solvent; and covers responsibilities to the PSO itself, to third parties and to regulators.

Chapter 5 – Insolvency: duties and responsibilities

This chapter deals separately with the special circumstances relating to appointees' liability in the event that a PSO becomes insolvent.

Chapter 6 – Protection from liability

This chapter examines the different forms of legal protection available to appointees, dependent on the legal status of their PSO.

Summary

S1 In its examination of local public spending bodies, the Committee on Standards in Public Life received evidence from witnesses and correspondents raising concerns about the personal legal liability of governors, board members and trustees of public bodies. There was a perception that the law lacked consistency in its treatment of those who serve voluntarily on such bodies, and that this might discourage people from offering their services.

S2 The Committee recommended that "the Government should seek to ensure broad consistency and adequate protection in respect of the personal liability of all appointed or elected members, directors, trustees and others responsible for bodies providing public services".[1]

S3 The Committee and the Government agreed that it would be sensible to commission legal research into the problem. This is a summary of the resultant study.

Definitions

S4 The study is concerned with public service organisations (PSOs), publicly funded organisations which provide public services on a non-profit-making basis. The body responsible for a PSO's governance is defined as its 'responsible body', and the individuals who serve on the responsible body are defined as its 'appointees'. The potential legal liability of these appointees is the principal focus of the study.

Organisations studied

S5 A wide range of PSOs has been examined, in order to ensure that the study covers all types of legal structure in current use by such organisations.

S6 Subjects of the study include National Health Service (NHS) trusts, universities, schools and further education colleges, training and enterprise councils and registered social landlords. Registered charities and non-departmental public bodies have also been included. The appointees who serve on these PSOs usually work on a part-time basis without financial reward.

S7 With one exception (local authority schools) the public services provided by local authorities and central government departments have not been included. However, the study does cover the potential liability of local authority nominees who serve on the responsible body of a PSO.

Legal structure

S8 The legal structure of a PSO determines the duties and responsibilities which are laid upon appointees, and influences the personal liabilities which they may incur.

S9 There are six types of legal structure in common and current use, details of which are set out fully in the study. They are:

Statutory corporations
Chartered corporations
Companies limited by guarantee
Industrial and provident societies
Trusts
Unincorporated associations

S10 The most important distinction for the purposes of the study is between corporate and non-corporate legal structures. The first four structures on the above list are corporate, the last two non-corporate.

---

[1]   Recommendation 45 *Local Public Spending Bodies* (May 1996) Cm 3270-I.

Corporate and non-corporate structures

S11 A corporate legal structure gives a PSO its own legal identity. It enables a PSO to do things that an ordinary person could do, e.g. enter into contracts, own property, sue and be sued, all in its own name. The responsible body of a PSO with a corporate structure directs its actions; but in law such actions are not those of individual appointees. They are those of the PSO itself.

S12 Non-corporate legal structures have no such legal identity. A PSO with a non-corporate structure must have someone to carry out all necessary actions on its behalf. Any action so taken on behalf of a non-corporate PSO is not regarded in law as the PSO's own action; it is the action of the individual or the group who took or authorised it. The persons most likely to be called upon to carry out these activities are the appointees to the responsible body (a PSO's employees may also perform these tasks, but the liability of employees is well established under employment and contract law, and is not studied here).

S13 Accordingly, appointees to responsible bodies of non-corporate PSOs are placed under a duty to act *in place of* the PSO, whereas corporate appointees are under a less onerous duty to act *on behalf of* the PSO. It follows that appointees in non-corporate structures are more likely to commit acts which may render them subject to a personal liability.

S14 Moreover, the lack of legal identity in a non-corporate PSO places appointees under direct legal responsibilities to regulatory bodies, and makes them directly subject to aspects of the civil and criminal law which regulate a PSO's activities. This further increases their potential personal liability, beyond that which attaches to appointees in corporate PSOs.

S15 For these reasons, the modern trend has been for PSOs to be established with a corporate structure. But this does have disadvantages, and there remain significant numbers of PSOs in the charities field with the non-corporate structures of trusts and unincorporated associations. They therefore have no separate legal personality. As a result there has been growing pressure to develop a new corporate structure for trusts and unincorporated associations in order to remove the additional risks of liability for appointees. A working group (comprising the National Council for Voluntary Organisations (NCVO), the Charity Law Association and Liverpool University) has been examining the case for reform, and has concluded that a new corporate structure is merited. This work is still in development.

S16 While appointees in corporate structures are usually better protected than their non-corporate counterparts, the precise benefit conferred by corporate status has been the subject of concern for appointees in some government sponsored PSOs. The question is presently unresolved whether appointees to such PSOs can be jointly liable with the PSO for its corporate acts.

Legal duties and responsibilities

S17 Common legal duties and responsibilities are placed upon all appointees, although their exact nature varies according to the PSO's legal structure. These duties are set out fully in the study, for both a solvent and an insolvent PSO, but in essence they comprise:[2]

(a) a duty to act with skill and care;
(b) fiduciary responsibilities;
(c) governance responsibilities; and
(d) responsibilities owed to third parties and regulators.

S18 The legal structure and governing instruments of each PSO (i.e. the founding documents which set out the PSO's purpose and how it is to be administered), together with the requirements of regulatory authorities, determine how these duties apply to appointees. Lay, professional and nominee appointees need to understand how

---

[2] These duties and responsibilities appear under a number of different names at law, but for ease of explanation and comparison these are the categories under which they have been studied.

these duties may vary because of their particular status. However, it will always be through an appointee's failure to exercise a duty properly that personal liability will arise.

S19 For the most part, the law will find such a failure only if appointees have acted in a manner which deserves the imposition of personal liability, i.e. have acted wrongfully or failed to display the standards which are reasonably required. For example, misappropriation of a PSO's assets, or acting recklessly or against advice when investing a PSO's funds, are types of behaviour which will leave an appointee personally responsible for the adverse consequences.

S20 However, potential liability can also arise where appointees have failed to understand their duties; or where the law specifies that an appointee has failed to perform a particular duty without having acted wrongfully or in bad faith, often known as a 'technical breach'.

S21 It is important that clear and comprehensive guidance on their legal duties and responsibilities is given to all appointees before they take up an appointment, to avoid their incurring personal liability through ignorance. This is particularly true of fiduciary and governance duties, where the governing instruments will set out clear rules by which the PSO is to be run. PSOs and their regulators have done considerable work to produce such guidance in recent years.

S22 However, it is difficult to offer appointees conclusive guidance on all aspects of their duties and responsibilities, because the standards of conduct required of them have not always been fully tested by the courts, particularly where PSOs have charitable status. For example, even where a PSO's legal structure is not a trust, the duty of skill and care placed upon appointees can often be the same as that of a trustee. While this may be an appropriately high standard of stewardship, there is no clear legal basis for such 'quasi-trustee' status. As a result these appointees may face problems over the legal interpretation of their duties and the forms of protection from liability that are available to them.

S23 The study shows that in certain rare circumstances some appointees run a risk of personal liability even where they have acted with the best of intentions. This can occur particularly in relation to the fiduciary and governance duties. For example, acting without the proper authority of the responsible body can render some appointees personally liable to a third party for any loss caused thereby. This liability can arise even where the appointee acted honestly, or the mistake was excusable. The risk of this rare liability arising will be reduced if appointees understand fully the terms of their governing instruments. Equally, appointees in PSOs with the structure of a company are not subject to the same risks in relation to unauthorised conduct as appointees in other corporate structures, and the study shows how the rules vary for the different structures.

Personal acts

S24 Appointees will naturally be liable for any wrongful acts they perform in their capacity as private citizens. However, the study explains that acts carried out in connection with duties to a PSO may also be treated, if wrongful under statute or common law, as the personal acts of appointees.

Insolvency

S25 Appointees' duties may be affected if a PSO is faced with possible or actual insolvency. For non-corporate appointees insolvency does not add to their duties, but it removes one of the main forms of protection that would otherwise relieve them from the consequences of liabilities incurred where they have acted in place of the PSO (i.e. indemnities from a PSO's funds).

S26 In corporate structures limited liability status allows appointees to avoid most personal consequences which might arise from a PSO's insolvency (unless the insolvency arises from an appointee's failure to fulfil their governance, skill and care, or fiduciary duties). However, the study highlights how appointees in companies and industrial and provident societies owe additional specific duties to third party creditors under the remedy of wrongful trading. The study concludes that neither statutory nor chartered corporations are subject to these provisions.

Protection

S27 In the absence of clear and tested relevant law on appointees' duties, and given the risk of 'technical breach', it is especially important that all appointees should be afforded protection against personal liability if their actions have been in good faith. Such protection can be provided by the courts or by PSOs, and can be divided into two types: protection which prevents a liability occurring and protection which relieves an appointee from the consequences of a liability.

S28 There are five ways at law in which protection can be afforded to an appointee to prevent a potential liability arising:

    (a) Statutory forms of relief;
    (b) Statutory forms of immunity;
    (c) Exclusion clauses;
    (d) Ratification of acts; and
    (e) Permission to bring proceedings.

S29 There are then two ways in law that appointees can be relieved from the consequences of liability:

    (a) Insurance; and
    (b) Indemnities.

S30 The study examines each of these different methods, and shows that the protection available to appointees varies between PSOs according to their legal structure and the attitudes of the regulatory authorities overseeing their activities.

S31 Only a minority of appointees (trustees and company directors) benefit from a statutory safeguard giving a court the discretion to grant relief to appointees who have acted honestly and reasonably, but find themselves facing a potential liability. No other appointees benefit from such a generous and general provision, although it has been suggested that a 'quasi-trustee' could so

benefit. The study concludes that the availability of such relief should not be relied upon by appointees other than company directors and true trustees.

S32 The provision of *immunity* from suit for appointees is rare, and where it does exist the courts have been inclined to limit its application. The other three methods of preventing a liability arising (exclusion clauses, ratification and permission to bring proceedings) can all assist appointees to reduce the risks of a liability arising where they have acted in good faith.

S33 In terms of the two types of protection which will relieve an appointee from the consequences of a personal liability, insurance and indemnities, there are problems with both.

S34 Only some PSOs are able legally to purchase personal liability *insurance* for appointees from the PSO's funds. While recognising that protecting appointees from the consequences of their wrongdoing is not desirable, the use of insurance need not give rise to unwarranted protection and can be a valuable form of reassurance for appointees.

S35 Where *indemnities* are offered to appointees a number of difficulties can arise. Indemnities are the main form of protection for appointees acting in place of a non-corporate PSO, yet they are worthless if the liability exceeds the assets of the PSO. Equally, an indemnity from the government is a major form of protection for appointees of PSOs which are prevented from taking out insurance (i.e. non-departmental public bodies). However, the study has concluded that the terms of this indemnity are not as generous as the commercial insurance policies that could be purchased for such appointees. Representatives of local authorities who are nominated to serve on the responsible body of a PSO are also unclear about the extent to which they can benefit from indemnities from their local authority. Recent case-law has caused much confusion on this issue, and it remains an unresolved problem.

Overall conclusions

S36 Legal liability is a complex issue, depending ultimately on the facts of any case. It is impossible for a study such as this to produce firm conclusions that will reassure all appointees that they can never be personally liable if they have acted in good faith. However, the study suggests that such instances will be rare. If appointees understand fully their duties and responsibilities, the risks of personal liability arising will be very substantially reduced.

S37 Since absolute reassurance on this subject is impossible, it is important that the types of protection provided to appointees are effective and equally available to all. They must also be justifiable in terms of the cost involved and the risk being covered. The study shows that this has yet to be achieved for all appointees.

Definitions

D1 Public service organisations (PSOs)

For convenience, the term 'public service organisation' (PSO) has been used in the study to embrace the particular range of organisations and institutions studied. This does not mean that all organisations providing public service are thereby included in its scope. For example, with the exception of local authority schools, organisations in local government providing public services (e.g. social services departments or libraries) have not been studied.

Those bodies that have been included possess all three of the following characteristics:

(a) **Their work consists of providing services for public benefit.**
This may include tangible benefits such as financial assistance or the supply of goods or housing, or those that are intangible such as the provision of care, advice or education.

(b) **They receive public funds (from central or local government) to assist them in carrying out this work.**
This includes organisations which are wholly or mainly dependent on such funding, as well as those with substantial or principal income from other sources.

(c) **They are non-profit-making organisations.**
This means that their purpose is to provide a public benefit and not to create wealth; and that any profits made from their activities are applied solely for that public benefit and are not available for other purposes or for distribution to third parties.

D2 The responsible body

There is an important distinction between the PSO itself as an organisation and the body responsible for its governance. Throughout the study, the term 'responsible body' is used to describe the governing or controlling group to which individuals are appointed or elected, and through which they have stewardship of a PSO's affairs.

In all cases the responsible body will carry out the practical tasks of governance for the organisation. However, the precise legal status of the responsible body varies. In some PSOs the responsible body will possess a particular legal structure (such as the governing body of a local authority school, which is a statutory corporation). In others, the responsible body will not be distinct, in legal terms, from the main legal structure of the PSO (for example, where a university is a chartered corporation its council is not a separate entity legally).

In this study, therefore, 'responsible body' means the group of people who exercise ultimate responsibility for the affairs and activities of a PSO, whether or not the two are legally distinct. 'PSO' means the organisation itself, as defined above.

D3 Appointees

The principal concern of this study is the people who give their time and effort, usually on a part-time basis and without financial reward, to serve on the responsible bodies of PSOs. They are charged with the stewardship of the organisation and bear ultimate responsibility for its affairs. They may be governors, directors, trustees or have other titles. Some are appointed, others elected or nominated.

However, in describing them collectively the word 'appointee' has been used throughout the study. The term has not been adopted simply for convenience, but because the more precise descriptions such as 'director' or 'trustee' are each associated in law with specific types of legal structure and responsibility. Therefore these specific designations have been used only in the appropriate legal context.

For the same reason, the term 'member' is used only if the legal context requires it. This distinction is explored more fully in Chapter 1.

D4 Regulators

A PSO may come under the aegis of a regulatory authority because of its legal structure, or because of the particular public service which it provides. Organisations which fund PSOs can also supply rules about how the PSO operates. The term 'regulator' has been used to describe organisations and authorities which oversee the activities of a PSO. For example, the Charity Commission, the funding councils for further and higher education and government departments overseeing non-departmental public bodies (NDPBs) all fall within this definition. The work of regulators in relation to appointees is discussed in Chapter 4, Section C.

D5 Governing instruments

The term 'governing instruments' is used to describe the documents which set out the PSO's purpose and how it is to be administered by the responsible body. The particular legal form of governing instruments will vary for different types of PSO, and will need to take account of the requirements of general law and of regulators.

Chapter 1 – Public service organisations

The PSOs

1.1 In selecting public service organisations for study, it has naturally not been possible to cover all those that fall within the definition of a PSO set out above.[3]

1.2 Instead, the study takes selected examples from the fields of education, housing and health in order to illustrate the variety of legal structures which PSOs may adopt. The examples studied are:

National Health Service (NHS) trusts
Registered social landlords[4]
Further education colleges
Universities[5]
Grant maintained schools
Local authority schools
Training and enterprise councils (TECs)

1.3 The study also looks at two classes of PSO:

Registered charities;[6] and
Non-departmental public bodies (NDPBs, familiarly known as quangos).[7]

These are somewhat different to the PSOs listed at paragraph 1.2 above, because they are not organisations providing a single type of public benefit, but are descriptive terms covering a wide range of institutions, which can, but need not, exist to provide public services, as defined above.

1.4 For example, some registered charities provide services for 'relief of the poor', which would fall within the study's definition of a PSO, but others provide services to secure 'the advancement of religion', which would not. However, for the purposes of the research, no attempt has been made to distinguish the different types of registered charity in terms of the public benefit to be secured, since the law on personal liability is not affected by such distinctions.

1.5 Non-departmental public bodies (NDPBs) can perform a variety of different functions for central government. They may be divided into three types: executive, advisory and tribunals. The first of these includes NDPBs which have administrative, regulatory and commercial functions,[8] the second provide advisory services to government,[9] and the third is essentially judicial in nature.[10] The latter two types are less likely to be organisations providing public benefit within the study's definition, and the research has looked exclusively at executive NDPBs (although it is accepted that even within this group, not every NDPB is a PSO).[11]

---

3   Definition D1, page 8 above.

4   Following the Housing Act 1996, the term 'registered social landlord' (RSL) is the correct legal term for housing associations registered with the Housing Corporation, and the study will use this term in preference to 'housing association'. See Appendix A for further details of this type of PSO, and the selection of RSLs for study.

5   Both pre-1992 and post-1992 – See Appendix A.

6   I.e. charities registered with the Charity Commission – see paragraph 3.43 below.

7   NHS trusts are a recognised form of NDPB, but have a distinct regime which sets them apart from other NDPBs. For this reason they have been treated separately for the purpose of the study.

8   E.g. the national museums, the Countryside Commission or the Commission for Racial Equality.

9   E.g. the Committee on Standards in Public Life, the Law Commission or the Committee on the Safety of Medicines.

10   E.g. the Criminal Injuries Compensation Board, the Immigration Appeals Tribunal or the Mental Health Review Tribunal.

11   For further details of NDPBs, their structure and their work see the Cabinet Office publications *NDPBs – A guide for Departments* (1992) as amended, and *Public Bodies 1997* The Stationery Office (Dec 1997).

Exclusions

1.6 With the exception of local authority schools, this study does not cover public services provided by central or local government. But it does consider the liability of local authority nominees who serve on the responsible bodies of the organisations listed at paragraph 1.2 above.[12] Nor does it cover ecclesiastical bodies.

Legal structures – the six classes

1.7 Every PSO must be underpinned by a legal structure, but not all structures are the same. The differences between them will determine the potential personal legal liability of appointees and each has advantages and disadvantages which will be examined in subsequent chapters.

1.8 For the purposes of the study, the relevant legal structures of PSOs are divided into six classes within two types. The two types are *corporate* and *non-corporate* structures.

1.9 Four of the classes are *corporate* structures:

> (a) Statutory corporations – created directly by Act of Parliament;
>
> (b) Chartered corporations – created by Royal Charter;
>
> (c) Companies limited by guarantee – registered under the Companies Acts 1985–89; and
>
> (d) Industrial and provident societies – registered under the Industrial and Provident Societies Act 1965.

1.10 The other two classes are *non-corporate* structures:

> (e) Trusts – created by deed; and
>
> (f) Unincorporated associations – created by contract.

Exclusions

1.11 The above classes do not exhaust the structures which can be used by PSOs, but they represent those which are most widespread and common. Excluded from the study are friendly societies, companies limited by shares and ecclesiastical corporations.

PSOs and legal structures – the assumptions

1.12 The list of PSOs at paragraph 1.2 above uses the ordinary names by which each PSO will be known to the public. However, the names conceal the fact that some of these PSOs can exist in a variety of legal forms. This means that, having produced a classification of legal structures, the study cannot neatly allot a particular structure to each named PSO. Instead, the research has had to accommodate the fact that institutions which provide the same type of public benefit, e.g. universities, will exist with different legal structures.

1.13 Accordingly, certain assumptions have been made about the structures used by the PSOs studied, in order to make the task of comparison easier. These are set out in Appendix A.

1.14 Appendix A also contains basic information about the characteristics of the PSOs studied, by way of background. The Committee's Second Report *Local Public Spending Bodies* also provides greater detail about the work of many of the PSOs studied.[13]

---

12   See Chapter 6 and Appendix E.

13   *Second Report of the Committee on Standards in Public Life* (May 1996) Cm 3270-I.

Chapter 2 – Appointees to PSOs

Introduction

2.1 This study is concerned only with appointees as previously defined,[14] and not with a PSO's salaried employees whose duties and liabilities will be regulated by a contract of employment and by employment law.

2.2 Most of the people covered by the study will regard themselves as volunteers. In general they work without financial reward other than out-of-pocket expenses, and give their time freely to the responsible body of a PSO.

2.3 Some appointees do receive limited remuneration (for details of which see Appendix B), and some will have been nominated to serve on a responsible body by reason of their principal paid employment or because of their public position. These factors can affect the legal position of appointees in terms of personal liability, or protection therefrom, and this is addressed in subsequent chapters.

2.4 The study assumes that all appointees who are the subject of this study have been properly and lawfully appointed to the PSOs they serve. Therefore, the study does not consider the different rules which govern the propriety of such appointments.

2.5 For the purposes of the study three types of appointee need to be distinguished, since their status affects the legal treatment of their potential liability. They are:

(a) The *lay appointee* who serves on a responsible body in a general capacity, and has no particular professional knowledge or expertise to bring to the work of the PSO;

(b) The *professional appointee* who, while not occupying a salaried position in the PSO, brings particular skills or professional knowledge to the PSO when sitting on its responsible body; and

(c) The *nominee appointee,* who is nominated by a third party to serve on the responsible body and to act as a representative of the nominating organisation (e.g. a local authority). Nomination therefore means more than simple recommendation for appointment, and in the study an individual will be described as a nominee appointee only if acting in such a representative capacity.

Method of appointment

2.6 Whether appointees are nominated, elected or chosen has no bearing on the legal treatment of potential personal liability. It may, however, affect the degree of legal protection which is available. Details of the appointment methods used by different PSOs are set out in Appendix A.

Membership

2.7 Most of the legal structures identified in the study need members to enable the PSO to function. Thus in the case of unincorporated associations the membership will comprise the individuals who set up or subscribe to the PSO, and who contract with one another to form the organisation.[15] However, membership is not just a practical requirement. It is a vital legal component of all corporate structures which allows a separate legal personality to be created for the PSO: the 'corporate body'.[16] Trusts are the only type of structure which do not have a membership requirement.

---

[14] See Definition D3, page 8 above.

[15] See paragraphs 3.38 ff below.

[16] This is not true for corporate structures which are 'corporations sole', which can exist with a single 'member'. However, corporations sole are not common, and no examples have been found of their use by PSOs.

2.8 Members themselves can have rights and liabilities in respect of their PSO solely by reason of their membership. For example, the members of a company limited by guarantee can control the PSO via general meetings and the members of a chartered corporation can, in theory, exercise control at equivalent meetings.[17]

2.9 However, membership need not bring with it responsibility for the day-to-day stewardship of a PSO. It will depend on the particular legal structure adopted. In some cases the only members of the PSO will be the appointees on the responsible body (e.g. in many FE colleges) so that all members bear equal responsibility for overseeing the PSO. In other cases the membership will be much wider (e.g. in many pre-1992 universities, where students and academics are members), but only certain members will have actual responsibility for the overall governance of the PSO.

2.10 Chapter 3 provides further details of the precise membership requirements for the different legal structures studied.

2.11 This study is concerned only with the responsible body through which the practical day-to-day stewardship of each PSO is exercised, and in which context potential questions of legal liability are most likely to arise. Therefore, members as such are not paid special attention.

Relinquishing appointment

2.12 The study focuses on the current appointees of a PSO. However, mention should be made here of the effect of the retirement or death of an appointee, in terms of their personal liability for acts undertaken while they served on a responsible body.

2.13 In general, appointees retain responsibility for the actions which they undertake while serving on a responsible body, even after their retirement. Therefore, where the chapters which follow identify conduct which gives rise to a potential liability, that liability can still arise after an appointee's retirement.[18] However, appointees cannot be liable for acts undertaken by their successors and in which they have had no involvement. Therefore, it is important for appointees to appreciate that retirement from a responsible body will not relieve them of responsibilities which accrue to them personally during their stewardship of a PSO.[19]

2.14 A similar principle applies upon the death of an appointee. As the rights and liabilities under discussion in this study are personal ones, they usually survive both for and against the estate of the deceased, and will be assumed by the personal representatives. In a few cases a cause of action will not survive the death of the appointee, for example if the case is one for alleged defamation by the appointee. However, in general, potential claims will not be extinguished by the death of an appointee.

---

[17] In practice, the rights and liabilities of members will depend upon the detailed terms of the governing instruments.

[18] But see also the discussion of limitation periods at page 66 below.

[19] Chapter 4 shows that such liabilities can arise from legitimate, *bona fide* acts (such as entering into a contract on behalf of a trust), as well as acts which involve wrongdoing.

Chapter 3 – The legal structures explained

Introduction

3.1 This chapter provides a short commentary on each of the six classes of legal structure identified in Chapter 1:

(a) The statutory corporation – created directly by Act of Parliament;

(b) The chartered corporation – created by Royal Charter;

(c) The company limited by guarantee – registered under the Companies Acts 1985–89;

(d) The industrial and provident society – registered under the Industrial and Provident Societies Act 1965;

(e) The trust – created by deed; and

(f) The unincorporated association – created by contract.

3.2 The commentary is selective and does not purport to represent a complete legal analysis of each structure. Instead, the commentary concentrates on the method of creation, and the elements of the structure of particular relevance to personal liability. The availability of limited liability status for PSOs is also discussed, to be developed in Chapter 5.

3.3 First, the distinction between the corporate and non-corporate structures needs to be explained.

Corporate and non-corporate structures

3.4 A legal structure is not the same thing as a legal personality. Possession of a legal personality confers an identity upon an organisation, with which it can assume rights, duties and liabilities.

3.5 For example, a PSO which possesses a legal personality can do many of the things that an ordinary person can do: own property in its own name, enter into contracts in its own name or defend legal proceedings in its own name.[20] These actions would, of course, be undertaken on behalf of the organisation by people authorised to do so. But the law would recognise the PSO, not the individuals who are taking the particular action, as the legal entity responsible for the consequences of each act.

3.6 PSOs which have corporate structures, either for themselves or for their responsible bodies, possess legal personalities.[21] PSOs with non-corporate structures do not (subject to an exception referred to at paragraph 3.36 below).

3.7 Therefore, PSOs with non-corporate structures cannot be held legally responsible, as organisations, for their actions. Instead, individuals (or other organisations which do possess legal personalities) must take responsibility at law for all the activities of a non-corporate PSO.

3.8 This makes a significant difference to the responsibilities of appointees to non-corporate PSOs, and consequently to the personal liability they may incur. This is considered fully in Chapter 4, Section A.

Limited liability

3.9 Another important difference between corporate and non-corporate structures is the ability of appointees in corporate structures to benefit from 'limited liability' status. This means that the liability of appointees to contribute toward the PSO's debts

---

[20] The precise powers of the legal personality will depend on the type of structure, and the governing instruments, as explained further below.

[21] The particular type of corporate legal structure of a PSO will determine whether the legal identity attaches to the responsible body or to the institution as a whole. Appendix A sets out the position for the different PSOs studied: e.g. local authority maintained schools as a whole have no corporate structure, but the governing body of every such school does (s.88 Education Act 1996). Conversely, a pre-1992 university normally includes a wide range of members, and it is the institution as a whole which is identified as the 'corporate body'. See also the discussion of membership in Chapter 2 above.

(in the event of insolvency) is restricted or, in the case of statutory and chartered corporations, removed altogether. The rationale for the restriction is that third party creditors should look to the assets of the corporate PSO, with its separate legal personality, and not the assets of the individual members of the responsible body.

3.10 This protection is available where a corporate PSO has been wound up or dissolved, rather than while the PSO is a going concern (it being unnecessary in the latter case since the PSO will be able to meet its liabilities). However, the protection afforded by limited liability status is modified by insolvency law which places certain duties (and potential liabilities) on appointees in some corporate structures. This is discussed fully in Chapter 5.

3.11 Non-corporate structures do not enjoy the automatic limited liability status from which corporate structures benefit. The internal rules of an unincorporated association can provide for how deficits are to be dealt with as between members, but such rules cannot restrict the rights of third parties against appointees.[22]

Corporate PSOs

3.12 The law recognises two classes of corporate structure: ecclesiastical and lay. Ecclesiastical corporations are not a subject of the study. The lay class can be further divided into civil and eleemosynary corporations. Statutory corporations, industrial and provident societies, and companies are lay corporations. Chartered corporations may be lay or eleemosynary, and the difference between them is discussed at paragraph 3.46 below, in the context of charitable structures.

Statutory Corporations:

Most NDPBs
NHS trusts
Post-1992 universities
Further education colleges
Grant maintained schools
Local authority schools

3.13 Parliament can confer a corporate structure on a PSO by providing in legislation that a group of persons (the members) will be a 'body corporate'.[23] The result is a statutory corporation. If the entity is to be a PSO it will be charged with providing a public benefit by the government.

3.14 While a statutory corporation has a separate legal personality, the basic legal rule is that a statutory corporation can only do what it is authorised to do by statute (expressly or by implication).[24] Thus, in addition to defining the public benefit, the relevant legislation will define the constitutional form of the PSO, its powers and its duties. These matters, set out in the primary legislation, can also be supplemented by subsequent regulations or directions promulgated by the Secretary of State under whose jurisdiction the activities of the PSO will fall; together these will determine the terms of the governing instruments. Statutory corporations do not enjoy Crown immunity.[25]

3.15 As a corporate structure, a statutory corporation has its own legal personality, and the appointees to its responsible body, usually known as governors or board members, will be the only members of the corporate body. In principle appointees in statutory corporations have no liability for the debts of the PSO.[26] Such protection could be removed by the governing instruments

---

[22] See Chapter 4, Section A, Duty 1 for details of how such liabilities can arise.

[23] While it is possible to create a statutory corporation by special Acts of Parliament (e.g. local Acts), they are rare, and of little relevance to PSOs. The study assumes that public general Acts of Parliament are the relevant form of legislation.

[24] This is in contrast with a chartered corporation which, at law, can do anything a natural person can do. See paragraph 3.18 below.

[25] Bodies which have Crown immunity are lawfully immune from criminal prosecution, or statutory controls, unless explicitly subjected to them (although it is government policy that no advantage should be taken of the criminal exception). However, in a recent House of Commons debate the Secretary of State for Health indicated that his department was examining the case for restoration of 'Crown indemnity' for NHS trusts: *Official Report* 297 col 636 (7 July 1997).

[26] Unlike in companies and industrial and provident societies these appointees do not contribute or guarantee a nominal sum to limit their liability, making their position one of 'no liability' rather than 'limited liability'.

of the corporation, but no PSO with the structure of a statutory corporation has been identified with such provisions.[27]

3.16 Secretaries of State are variously given rights to dissolve statutory corporations or approve their discontinuance, subject to duties of consultation. The procedures laid down in the relevant legislation are the only methods by which such corporations may be terminated.[28]

Chartered corporations:

Pre-1992 universities
Some NDPBs

3.17 The Crown, acting through the auspices of the Privy Council, can create a corporate structure by conferring a Royal Charter upon a PSO. Some PSOs are created at origin as chartered corporations, others have the Royal Charter conferred on them at a later date.

3.18 In either case, the charter makes a PSO subject to a particular set of laws specifically designed to regulate its affairs (often referred to as a form of domestic statute).[29] The scope of public benefit and the PSO's powers and duties are laid down in the charter. However, a chartered corporation differs from a statutory corporation since "generally speaking, such a corporation can do anything that an ordinary individual may do".[30] Thus, its separate legal personality is unfettered by its governing instruments as far as its relationship with third parties is concerned. This also modifies the application of the '*ultra vires*' rule, a subject that is discussed in Chapter 4, Section A.

3.19 Unlike statutory corporations, the members of the corporate body are not restricted to the responsible body, and in the case of a university would usually include staff and graduates. Appointees to chartered corporations (often called council members) benefit from limited liability as members of the corporate body, as far as the PSO's debts to a third party are concerned.

3.20 Despite the grant of a Royal Charter, chartered corporations do not have Crown immunity.[31] As with statutory corporations, appointees are automatically afforded the protection of 'no liability' for the debts of the PSO, unless the charter specifies otherwise.[32]

3.21 A charter can be surrendered voluntarily by the corporation, forfeited or revoked. Revocation will usually be achieved by Act of Parliament.[33]

Companies limited by guarantee:

TECs
Some registered charities
Some NDPBs

3.22 A company limited by guarantee is created by registration under the Companies Acts 1985–89. It is also possible to register companies limited by shares, but the study does not consider this structure since shareholding is more appropriate to organisations set up to make and distribute profits. Accordingly, where the term 'company' is used in the study, it means a company limited by guarantee.[34] The public benefit to be secured by the company (its objects), its constitution, powers and duties will be set out in the company's

---

[27] See *Halsbury's Laws of England* 4th ed Vol 9 para 1209.

[28] For a discussion of the relationship between the law of insolvency and statutory corporations see Chapter 5 and Appendix D below.

[29] These domestic statutes are subject to the jurisdiction of a visitor, rather than the ordinary courts. See paragraphs C9 ff for further details of visitation.

[30] Per Bennet J in *Attorney General v Leicester Corporation* [1943] 1 Ch 86 at 93. Even where a charter specifically prohibits a particular act, the act is valid as against third parties (i.e. non-members of the corporation), although the charter may be revoked as a consequence, or an injunction obtained by a member to restrain the act (see *Halsbury's Laws of England* 4th ed Vol 9 para 1332).

[31] See *BBC v Johns* [1964] 1 All ER 923 and footnote 25 above.

[32] See *Halsbury's Laws of England* 4th ed Vol 9 para 1209.

[33] For further details of the different methods of dissolution see paragraph 5.7 below, and Appendix D on how this relates to insolvency.

[34] Unlimited companies and partnerships have not been studied, no examples of this type of PSO having been identified.

memorandum and articles of association which have to be drawn up in order to secure registration. Like statutory corporations, a company can only do those things which are within its objects and powers. Therefore, while it has a separate legal personality it does not have the capacity of a natural person.[35]

3.23 Appointees will usually be directors, and simultaneously members of the company (although there may be members who are not directors). The structure confers limited liability on all members by requiring them each to guarantee the debts of the company up to a nominal limit, usually £1.[36] As explained in Chapter 5, however, companies are one of the two legal structures (the other being industrial and provident societies) where limited liability status is modified by insolvency law.

3.24 Dissolution of a company structure is governed by company and insolvency law, and may be achieved by agreement of the members of the company, or by order of the court.

3.25 Some PSO companies are 'charitable companies', for which see paragraph 3.48 below.

Industrial and provident societies:

Registered social landlords

3.26 A PSO can register itself with the Registrar of Friendly Societies as an industrial and provident society under the Industrial and Provident Societies Act 1965. To qualify for registration it must be a bona fide co-operative society or established to carry on an industry, business or trade for the benefit of the community. Many such PSOs were formerly unincorporated associations which adopted industrial and provident society status to secure the advantages of a corporate structure.

3.27 The rules of the PSO under this structure must define the public benefit to be achieved and the powers and duties of members and the executive committee.[37] Like statutory corporations and companies, industrial and provident societies only have power to act in accordance with the governing instruments of the society. Thus, their legal personality is defined by such rules, and is not that of a natural person.

3.28 The membership of an industrial and provident society will frequently be wider than the responsible body, and limited liability status is available to the members, including the appointees (usually called 'committee members'). The liability of members upon dissolution of a society is limited to the outstanding value of the member's subscription.[38] While industrial and provident societies are not generally subject to company law, certain provisions of insolvency law do apply when a society is to be wound up (as opposed to being voluntarily dissolved),[39] for which see Chapter 5 below.

Non-corporate PSOs

3.29 There are only two classes of non-corporate structure which need to be considered in the study: trusts and unincorporated associations.

Trusts created by deed:

Some registered charities

3.30 The trust structure has been used for centuries in order to secure either public or private benefit.

---

[35] But see Chapter 4 paragraph A133 ff below on how the Companies Act 1985 (as amended) affects the capacity of a company when dealing with third parties.

[36] See s.74 Insolvency Act 1986 on the limited liability of members of the corporation in the event of an insolvent winding up.

[37] Industrial and Provident Societies Act 1965 s.1 (b), Sch.1.

[38] The unpaid sum on any shares; usually a nominal sum for PSOs (see also Industrial and Provident Societies Act 1965 ss.3 and 57).

[39] Industrial and Provident Societies Act 1965 ss.55 and 58 and *Re Norse Self Build Association Ltd* (1985) 1 BCC 99.

Trusts are created at the behest of a benefactor (for example an individual, a family or a company) who seeks to safeguard particular property or assets (capital) and see them or income from them applied for a specific beneficiary or purpose.[40] Where this purpose is for private benefit (i.e. of named beneficiaries), the creation and execution of the trust is regulated solely by the law of trusts, which is derived both from statute and case law.

3.31 Where the purpose is that of public benefit, as in the case of PSOs, the law of trusts will be combined with the law of charity. Together they will determine how the trust is created and run. As a non-corporate structure a trust has no separate identity at law.

3.32 For a PSO to be a valid trust the founding documents (the 'trust deed') will specify the public benefit to be achieved and the beneficiaries (who may be a class of people for a registered charity). It must also identify the individual trustees to whom responsibility for carrying out this work will be entrusted – the responsible body.

3.33 A trust requires no registration to give it legal effect, and may be created without falling within any specific system of regulation. In practice, the PSOs in this study which are trusts will be registered with the Charity Commission (see below). The trust structure can confer no limited liability as such upon trustees.

3.34 The essence of a PSO with a trust structure is that the general property and assets of the PSO are held on trust, and the organisation itself has status as 'a trust'. This needs to be distinguished from cases where a PSO with another legal structure, e.g. a statutory corporation, holds specific property on trust, as a result of a bequest or gift. In this latter situation the PSO itself will be the trustee in relation to that specific sum of money, or item of property, rather than the individual appointees. This situation will not alter the underlying legal structure of the non-trust PSO. Thus, the study ignores instances of specific property held on trust for the purpose of comparing PSOs, but recognises that PSOs may have dealings with trusts even where they have a different legal structure. NHS trusts are not trusts in the legal sense but are statutory corporations.

3.35 Termination of a trust will occur where the trust fund is exhausted, although it is possible for the underlying assets of a trust to be protected, and for trustees to be given powers only to use the income from the assets (e.g. the trust has a permanent endowment). This makes it less likely that the fund can ever run out. However, where a trust for charitable purposes is solvent, but circumstances change, the courts have extensive jurisdiction to alter the trust, transfer its assets, and take other steps to ensure the effective use of the funds which are the subject of the trust, under the *cy-près* doctrine.[41]

Intermediate structure

3.36 One exception to the principle that trusts have no separate legal personality needs to be noted. A certificate of incorporation can be granted by the Charity Commission to trustees of trusts which are registered as charities. This process has existed since 1872, although it has been simplified in recent years.[42]

3.37 A certificate of incorporation allows the trustees to carry out under a collective name some of the activities which a corporate structure can undertake. Thus to a limited extent the trustees acquire a separate legal identity. However, the certificate expressly confers no limited liability upon,

---

[40] The use of trust funds by commercial organisations for investment purposes is not included within this definition.

[41] See *Tudor on Charities* (8th ed 1995) chap 11. The doctrine is not relevant to non-charitable trusts, but as stated the study is concerned with trust PSOs which will be charitable.

[42] See ss.50–62 Charities Act 1993.

nor offers any other form of protection to, the trustees. Therefore, in terms of personal liability, the certificate makes no difference to the position of the trustee.[43] For the purposes of the study therefore, this intermediate structure has not been included.

Unincorporated associations created by contract:

Some registered charities

3.38 A PSO can adopt the structure of an unincorporated association with very little formality. All that is required is a set of rules which form a legally-binding contract between the people who have set up the PSO (the members). This type of structure is used by many small PSOs providing benefit on a local rather than a national scale, and is used by many registered charities. The appointees will be drawn from the membership (usually elected), often known as committee members.

3.39 Since the basis of the relationship is contractual,[44] there is no statutory requirement of registration and, indeed, no statutory regulation of unincorporated associations as a class of organisation. The rules of the association will specify the public benefit to be secured, but as a non-corporate body these rules are for regulating the relationship between members and do not affect third parties, as they would if it were a corporate body.

3.40 As a non-corporate structure, an unincorporated association has no separate legal identity. Unless the rules state otherwise, members of an unincorporated association are not liable to pay anything to the association, or third parties, beyond any annual subscription.[45] However, as explained in Chapter 4 below, this will not be the case where appointees are carrying out activities in place of the association.

3.41 Unincorporated associations can be dissolved voluntarily by a member's resolution, or by order of the court,[46] but insolvency law has no application to the dissolution.

Charitable status

3.42 It will be apparent that any consideration of the legal position of PSOs and their appointees must take account of the fact that many of them are charities. Charitable status is available to any PSO whose services fall within a class of activity that is legally prescribed as 'charitable', and which comes within the inherent 'charitable jurisdiction' of the courts.[47] It is beyond the scope of this study to engage in a detailed exposition of charity law as it applies to PSOs. Rather, the study concentrates on those aspects of charitable status which affect the question of personal liability.

3.43 A PSO can be registered with the Charity Commission as a charity, or it can be granted status as an exempt charity. Neither route is a means of establishing a PSO: instead it merely

---

43 In the course of the research it has been suggested that the certificate of incorporation may, in practice, limit trustee liability. In particular, questions have been raised about how such incorporation affects the contractual liability of trustees who would be able to sign contracts in the corporate name. The terms of section 54 of the Charities Act 1993 are clear: "All trustees notwithstanding their incorporation, shall be ... answerable and accountable for their own acts, receipts, neglects, and defaults, and for the due administration of the charity ... in the same manner and to the same extent as if no such incorporation had been effected"; and in the absence of a court case to test the point, the express terms of section 54 are assumed to prevail over the normal rules applying to incorporated bodies.

44 There has been much debate about the legal basis of the unincorporated association, and, in particular, how it holds its property (see for example the commentary in Warburton *Unincorporated Associations* (2nd ed 1992) chap 5). The courts have tended to adopt the contractual basis as the preferred analysis (*Re Recher's Will Trust* 1972 Ch 526), although it will ultimately be a question of fact in every case. In this study, it is assumed that appointees are subject to this contractual relationship, and are not trustees in the true sense of the word.

45 *Wise v Perpetual Trustee Co Ltd* [1903] AC 139.

46 *Re Lead Company's Workmen's Fund Society* [1904] 2 Ch 196.

47 There are four heads of charity: relief of poverty, human suffering and distress; advancement of religion; advancement of education; and publicly beneficial purposes. The jurisdiction of the court to monitor and control charities has existed from the earliest times, and while it originally depended on the presence of a trust, it is now exercisable in relation to corporations or companies. See the discussion in *Tudor on Charities* (8th ed 1995) pp 324–8.

recognises that the purposes of the PSO are charitable in law, entitling it to the various fiscal and presentational benefits enjoyed by charities.[48] An exempt charity is one which does not come within the regulatory jurisdiction of the Charity Commission because it is already adequately regulated by another outside body,[49] and such exempt charities are listed in Schedule 2 to the Charities Act 1993. Most of the PSOs studied fall into one of these categories, as noted in Appendix A.

3.44 As discussed above in the context of the trust, a distinction must be made between a PSO which is itself a charity (whether registered or exempt) with its general property held for exclusively charitable purposes, and a PSO which controls a separate charitable fund. Such a fund may be registered with the Charity Commission in its own right, but this does not render the PSO a charity.[50] The study is concerned with the structure of the organisation, and not individual bequests which it may control.

3.45 At law, the effect of charitable status upon the appointees to a PSO is not always clear. Such status does not alter the basic legal structure which controls how each PSO is governed, unless it is a 'charitable company' (see paragraph 3.48 below). But in practice appointees will find that charitable status confers additional duties and responsibilities upon them, and consequently further potential liabilities. This situation and the problems it causes are examined fully in Chapter 4 below.

Eleemosynary corporations

3.46 In the context of charities the position of eleemosynary corporations needs to be discussed. The classic definition of an eleemosynary corporation is an institution which is "established for the perpetual distribution of the free alms or bounty of the founder, to such person as he has directed".[51] The pre-1992 universities which are chartered corporations are the best known example of this type of corporation.

3.47 Unlike statutory corporations or companies, which are both civil corporations,[52] eleemosynary corporations hold their general property on charitable trust. This makes the corporate body (with its separate legal personality) a true trustee. However, it does not make the individual appointees true trustees, although they will owe a duty to the PSO to see that the terms of the trust are obeyed.[53] Eleemosynary corporations are subject to visitation,[54] and the role of the visitor is discussed in Chapter 4, Section C below.

Charitable companies

3.48 A charitable company is formed in the same manner as an ordinary company but, because it is registered with the Charity Commission, is treated differently by the law. Nevertheless, a company (such as a TEC) can exist for public benefit without being so registered, and is therefore not a charitable company in the legal sense.

3.49 Both types of company are considered in the succeeding chapters.

---

[48] Although reference is sometimes made to 'charitable corporations' (see for example Picarda *The Law and Practice Relating to Charities* (2nd ed 1995) chap 31) these have not been included in the study since the term does not represent a separate legal structure. For eleemosynary corporations see paragraph 3.46 below.

[49] Certain limited aspects of the Charity Commission's jurisdiction do apply to exempt charities. Of relevance to this study are (a) the right of appointees to approach the Charity Commission for advice in the event that they are in doubt about the legality of a proposed course of action (see ss.26 and 29 Charities Act 1993); and (b) the sanctioning of ex gratia payments (s.27 Charities Act 1993).

[50] Local authority schools and NHS trusts are examples of PSOs which do not have charitable status, but which often control some charitable funds.

[51] Warburton *Tudor on Charities* (8th ed 1995) p371, referring to Shelford *Law of Mortmain* (1836) 23.

[52] See paragraph 3.12 above.

[53] See paragraph A122 below.

[54] See *Tudor on Charities op cit* for a full description of the law of visitation, and paragraph C9 ff below for a brief summary.

Chapter 4 – The solvent PSO: duties and responsibilities

Introduction

4.1 Appointees need to understand their duties and responsibilities to assess the potential liability which can arise from their position. This chapter considers the duties owed by appointees to their PSO and to third parties in the context of a solvent PSO. Chapter 5 deals with duties which may additionally be owed when a PSO becomes insolvent.

4.2 Having outlined such duties, this chapter discusses the potential liability in relation to each duty, although the question of whether the liability will actually arise will also depend on issues relating to protection from liability, which are dealt with in Chapter 6.

Sources of law

4.3 An appointee's duties and responsibilities will be derived from two overlapping sources: *the general law* and *the governing instruments* of each PSO.

4.4 The *general law* will be concerned with three matters: the legal structure of the PSO, the particular type of public benefit being provided, and the role performed by the PSO in society at large (i.e. as an employer or an occupier of land). These will combine to produce a body of law that defines the role of the appointee. It may not always be clear or consistent.

4.5 In addition to the general law, any study of the personal liability of appointees has to consider the particular *governing instruments* under which the PSO operates. These will define, amongst other things, the particular public service to be provided by the PSO and the powers the responsible body can exercise to provide such service. The particular importance of governing instruments is that they can redefine the role of the appointee as set out by the general law. In some cases a general law duty will be reinforced by the governing

instruments, while in other cases it will be relaxed or removed altogether.

4.6 A study of this scale cannot cover the individual details of every governing instrument which exists for the PSOs studied. Therefore, the study cannot define the exact position of every class of appointee in every PSO. However, the regulators and funders of PSOs usually require certain mandatory terms to be included in a PSO's governing instruments, and there are model instruments which PSOs are advised to follow. Reference will be made to these where appropriate, and the study takes as much account as possible of the particular circumstances of different PSOs.

The duties owed

4.7 The duties owed by appointees are examined under three headings:

Responsibilities owed to the PSO itself – Part A;

Responsibilities owed to third parties generally – Part B; and

Responsibilities owed to regulators – Part C.

4.8 Before turning to these particular duties, the question of joint and several liability needs to be discussed briefly.

Joint and several liability

4.9 It is assumed in this study that the conduct of an individual appointee is at issue. Therefore, in discussing potential liability the study focuses on the position of the single appointee. However, where a number of appointees participate in conduct which this study indicates may lead to personal liability, the law provides that all these individuals are jointly and severally liable. This means that each of the appointees is personally liable for the *whole* loss caused by the collective conduct, regardless of the degree of blame which can be attached to the individual. Further, they can be sued individually or collectively.

4.10 This harsh rule has been tempered by statute[55] and by equitable rules of contribution.[56] These give rights to an individual to recover contributions from another person in circumstances where the other person was not made subject to the original liability, but is, in fact, also responsible.

4.11 No further mention of joint and several liability will be made in the text, and appointees' duties will be discussed in the context of an individual appointee's conduct.

Section A – Responsibilities owed to the PSO

Introduction

A1 The responsibilities which an appointee owes to a PSO can be divided into five categories:

   (a) A duty to act for the PSO;
   (b) A duty of skill and care;
   (c) Fiduciary responsibilities;
   (d) Governance responsibilities; and
   (e) Responsibility for the acts of others.

A2 The law dealing with these different duties is complex and, in some cases, poorly developed. The following paragraphs explain, as far as it is known, the legal position of appointees under each heading, and the potential liability which can arise thereby.

A3 Where appropriate, this section also considers any law reform proposals which might affect appointees.

DUTY ONE: The duty to act for the PSO

Overview

A4 The duty to act for the PSO does not refer to the appointee's duty to have proper authority to carry out an act for the PSO (this is dealt with separately in Duty Four below). Rather, it covers the degree to which the appointee is required to interpose in the affairs of the PSO, and take personal responsibility for them.

A5 The important distinction between corporate and non-corporate structures has been explained in Chapter 3.[57] This distinction produces a set of responsibilities for appointees to non-corporate PSOs which do not exist for corporate PSOs. This is

---

[55] Civil Liability (Contribution) Act 1978.

[56] E.g. trustees who are sued individually may claim a contribution from co-trustees who have joined in a breach of trust (unless fraud is involved).

[57] See paragraphs 3.4 ff above.

because an appointee to a corporate body can act 'on behalf of' the PSO, whereas an appointee to a non-corporate body must act 'in place of' the PSO.

The general legal position

A6   A PSO's activities will usually require it to enter into contracts for the purchase of goods, enter into leases for the occupation of premises and employ staff to perform tasks. A corporate PSO is recognised at law as being able to undertake all of these activities. But it has no physical form by which to undertake the work, so it requires natural persons to do so on its behalf. Provided an appointee acting in this manner is properly authorised, this requirement places no responsibility on the appointee, beyond that of physically carrying through the transaction.[58] To put it another way, the identity of the appointee is not relevant to the activity – they stand as no more than a cipher for the PSO.

A7   An appointee in a non-corporate PSO has a responsibility that is far more burdensome than that just described for corporate appointees. Without a legal personality, the PSO needs the appointee to act as the principal in any transaction it wishes to undertake. Thus, the participation of the appointee is vital to the activity actually taking legal effect. The appointee will enter into the particular transaction in order to achieve something the PSO wants achieved, but the PSO will never appear as a character in the story.

A8   This will be the case for trust PSOs, where trustees acting for the purpose of the PSO will always act as principal.[59]

A9   For unincorporated associations, where a committee member acts for the purpose of the association, the position is a little more complicated. Such appointees still have no separate legal personality, but it will be a question of fact in every case whether they have acted as principal, as agents for the responsible body, or as agents for the wider membership of the unincorporated association. In most circumstances the liability will fall upon those members of the association who have authorised the action giving rise to the obligation (and this will usually be the responsible body).[60] Thus, while this question of fact will affect the extent of any liability placed on appointees it does not alter the basic responsibility of the committee members where they carry out transactions in place of the PSO.

Potential liability

A10   It will be obvious from the above discussion that liabilities arise for appointees in non-corporate structures as a result of this responsibility, where they will not exist for appointees to corporate PSOs. For a potential liability to arise there need be no breach of a duty, nor act of bad faith. For example, money will become due under contracts as a matter of course, and responsibility for payment in the first instance falls to the individuals who have entered into the contract. The potential liability exists purely and simply because appointees have undertaken on their own behalf to enter into relations with a third party to achieve the ends of the PSO.

A11   While this duty is a duty that is owed to the PSO, the consequences of undertaking it will frequently result in potential liabilities to third parties, e.g. under the contract which the appointee has signed, or the lease entered into. The nature of the liability will be determined by the particulars of the transaction involved. It may be a liability to perform a contract or to pay a sum of money. However, there are special kinds of relief available to non-corporate appointees from these liabilities

---

[58]   It is recognised that in larger PSOs employees may be carrying out these activities for the responsible body, under delegated authority. The study focuses on appointees who are themselves undertaking tasks for the PSO, in the absence of (a) powers to delegate or (b) employees.

[59]   As explained in Chapter 3 paragraphs 3.36 ff, trusts can avail themselves of an 'intermediate structure', which gives them a legal personality with which to perform tasks. However, the liability is still regarded as that of the trustees.

[60]   See for example *Bradley Egg Farms v Clifford* [1943] 2 All ER 378.

(in the form of indemnities). These are discussed in detail in Chapter 6, Section B below.

A12 There is also potential for 'social regulation', and the requirements of regulators to impose liabilities upon non-corporate appointees, because they are acting in place of the PSO, and these are discussed in Sections B and C below.

Law reform proposals

A13 For some time the position of the non-corporate appointee has been of concern to organisations providing public services and to their advisers.

A14 While there are a number of corporate structures available, they are not always appropriate for PSOs, particularly small ones. Both the company and the industrial and provident society require financial resources to create and maintain the legal structure, as well as administrative requirements that can be burdensome. As shown in Section C below, there can also be overlap between regulators where a PSO is a registered charity and has a corporate structure.

A15 The Deakin Report highlighted these problems in 1996,[61] and since then work has been undertaken to develop a new legal structure which would be corporate and confer limited liability upon appointees.[62] There would then be a means for existing non-corporate PSOs to convert to the new structure.

A16 The Charity Commission Report for 1996 reviewed work on the present proposals (at paragraphs 28 and 29), and it is understood that further consultations are taking place before draft primary legislation is developed.

Conclusions

A17 The duty to act in place of a non-corporate PSO is an onerous one. It can give rise to personal liability without any wrongdoing on the part of appointees. Although there is protection available for such appointees, in the form of indemnities, these operate after the liability has arisen, and will be of no value if the liability exceeds the assets of the PSO (as described fully in Chapter 6).

A18 Accordingly, appointees in non-corporate structures are under a greater burden than their counterparts in corporate structures. Such appointees need to appreciate the particular role they will be undertaking, namely to act in place of the PSO and the liabilities that can arise thereby. Equally, PSOs need to give consideration to employing a corporate structure wherever possible, although for smaller PSOs the existing forms of corporate structure are not always appropriate.

DUTY TWO: The duty to act with skill and care

Overview

A19 All appointees must act with skill and care when carrying out the stewardship of a PSO, but to discharge this duty to the PSO properly they need to understand the degree of skill (i.e. the expertise, experience or ability to be used when carrying out a particular task) and the amount of care (i.e. the attention and interest paid to that task) that they will be expected to exercise.

A20 It is important for appointees to appreciate that the law can require them to act using not just the skill they possess, or the care which they think is appropriate, but with the skill and care that the law decides they ought to have possessed or should have used. In other words, appointees can be judged by reference to an objective 'model' appointee, created by the courts. The following paragraphs explain what appointees need to know about the model which is relevant to them.

---

61 *Meeting the challenge of change: voluntary action into the 21st century* – The report of the Commission on the Future of the Voluntary Sector, NCVO Publications (1996) paragraphs 3.4.1–3.

62 This work has been undertaken as a joint project by the National Council for Voluntary Organisations, the Charity Law Association and Liverpool University.

A21 There is a considerable body of law, developed mainly by judges, on the duty of skill and care required of two types of appointee: the company director and the trustee. Unfortunately for appointees in PSOs with other legal structures, there is very little law dealing with their duty in this respect. This means that guidance for appointees in these PSOs is based on analogy, rather than definite law, and this can lead to confusion.

A22 Before considering the analogies which have been developed for other legal structures, the law on directors' and trustees' skill and care duties will be examined.

The skill and care of a company director

A23 The duty of skill and care required from a company director is still being developed by the courts today. Although the modern law in this area is often formulated in the context of a company undertaking activities for profit, the approach taken by the courts to directors of such companies is relevant in a study of PSOs.

A24 Traditionally, non-executive directors (NEDs)[63] have been expected to display only such skill as they actually possess, and to take such care as an ordinary person might reasonably be expected to take on their own behalf.[64] Therefore, professional appointees occupying the position of a non-executive director will be expected to apply their particular ability or experience when carrying out tasks for the responsible body, but lay appointees acting as non-executive directors will be required only to display such skill as they actually possess. They will not be compared with professional appointees.[65]

A25 Therefore, the model against which the director will be judged is partly based on the actual qualities of the individual (the skill), and partly based on 'the ordinary person acting on their own behalf' (the care). The particular qualities which a director possesses are therefore important in assessing the standard of a director's conduct under this duty.

A26 Errors of judgement (which the ordinary person could make) will not constitute a want of care. Equally, a non-executive director need not devote continuous attention to the affairs of the company; theirs is a part-time role. They may rely upon expert advice, and place trust in fellow directors to whom tasks are delegated. However, non-executive directors must continue to exercise their own judgement when taking advice and must not abdicate all responsibility for overseeing the conduct of others.[66]

A27 This summary of the law needs to be qualified in two respects.

A28 First, a new statute-based duty of skill and care has been created for company directors in situations where the company is heading for insolvency. The duty requires that a director displays the skill and care which can be expected of a reasonably diligent person carrying on the particular director's duties, as well as the skill and care which the director actually possesses. Therefore, under the new statutory test the director's subjective level of skill is only relevant if it improves upon the standard of the reasonable director; whereas under the traditional approach, the director's subjective level of skill is the starting point for setting the standard.[67] The former is a higher

---

[63] I.e. those directors who are not salaried (contracted) employees of the company, and are therefore akin to appointees on the responsible body of a PSO, although, in the commercial world, NEDs will usually receive remuneration.

[64] The classic case setting out the principles governing a director's duties in this regard is *Re City Equitable Fire Insurance* [1925] Ch 407, in the judgment of Romer J. For a recent case discussing this duty, see *Dorchester Finance Co Ltd v Stebbing* [1989] BCLC 498. For a detailed discussion of this aspect of a director's duties see *Palmer's Company Law* (looseleaf work) vol 2 part 8, para 8.4 ff.

[65] It is assumed in this analysis that professional appointees are not being legally employed in their professional capacity to advise the PSO; rather the skill and care duty attaches to their ordinary services for the responsible body.

[66] See also *Re Brazilian Rubber Plantation and Estates Ltd* [1911] 1 Ch 425 (per Neville J); and the discussion in *Palmer's Company Law op cit*. On the question of attendance at meetings, some governing instruments specify that appointees will be disqualified from office, if they fail to attend meetings for a certain period, without consent: see for example the provision for grant maintained schools at paragraph 23 of their Instrument of Government: Schedule 1, the Education (GM Schools) (Initial Governing Instruments) Regulations 1993, as amended.

[67] See *Gower's Principles of Modern Company Law* Davies (6th ed 1997) p642.

standard than the latter, and is considered fully in Chapter 5 below, in the context of an insolvent PSO.

A29 However, it should be noted that two recent judicial decisions have suggested that this standard is the one that should be applied to executive directors of a going concern, as well as an insolvent one.[68] If this view of the law is followed for non-executive directors in the future, then directors of PSO companies will always be judged by the higher standard of skill and care.

A30 Second, the growth of salaried company directors, and the introduction of new (non-legal) standards into the boardroom as a result of corporate governance reviews in the 1990s (e.g. the Cadbury Report, the Greenbury Report and the Hampel Report[69]), mean that there is a groundswell of opinion that the conduct of directors (particularly remunerated directors) should be judged by higher standards than those outlined above. While this movement has focused on salaried directors rather than non-executive appointees to PSOs, it has prompted the view that non-executive directors (of for profit organisations) should no longer see themselves as "mere figureheads".[70]

A31 These changes make it increasingly less certain that courts will abide by the traditional, less onerous, approach to the duty of skill and care for directors in the future.

The skill and care of a trustee

A32 The skill and care duties of a trustee are frequently described as being 'higher' than those of a company director. Even with the modern developments described above, this is still an accurate description, although the gap between the two is probably decreasing.[71]

A33 The model against which a trustee is judged is a more cautious one than that used for the director of a company.[72] The basic duty is to take such care as would an ordinary prudent person of business in relation to their own affairs.[73] With respect to some activities, however, the standard becomes still more demanding. For example, in relation to investments, the duty is to take the care that a prudent business person would take if acting for a person for whom they felt morally obliged to provide.[74]

A34 The use of the word 'prudence' in relation to a trustee is the key to their duty of care. Theirs is not a duty to take risks, and to be honest and sincere is not enough.[75] It is expected that trustees will act reasonably and prudently, and devote as much time as is necessary to the performance of their tasks on behalf of the PSO. Thus, a trustee is not in a position which the law would describe as 'part-time' as is the case for non-executive company directors. However, errors of judgement will not amount to a breach of the duty.[76] Trustees' reliance on expert advice and on their fellow trustees must be reasonable, as judged against an ordinary prudent person.

---

[68] See *Norman v Theodore Goddard* [1991] BCLC 1028 and *Re D'Jan of London* [1993] BCC 646, both decisions of Hoffmann LJ.

[69] Cadbury, May 1992; Greenbury, July 1995; Hampel, August 1997.

[70] *Gower's Principles of Modern Company Law* ibid p640.

[71] And see paragraph A39 ff below on the position of charitable companies.

[72] This duty, developed by the courts of equity, can be modified by the governing instruments of a trust, but it is assumed that a PSO will not alter the duty so as to lower it in relation to the skill and care required.

[73] *Speight v Gaunt* (1883) 9 App Cas 1 and *Re Luckings Will Trust* [1968] 1 WLR 866.

[74] See *Learoyd v Whiteley* (1887) 12 App Cas 727. Investment powers and duties of trustees are now regulated by the Trustee Investment Act 1961, in addition to any express terms in the governing instruments.

[75] *Cowan v Scargill* [1985] Ch 270.

[76] See discussion in *Underhill and Hayton Law of Trusts and Trustees* (15th ed 1995) pp 552–3.

A35 The skills which trustees ought to display remain those which they actually possess, so that professional appointees occupying the position of trustee will be expected to exercise such skills as they possess. As with directors, the duty assumes that the professional trustee is not being paid to undertake particular professional services for the trust. Indeed, where a trustee (lay or professional) is paid, higher standards apply.[77]

The quasi-trustee

A36 While the law is well developed for trustees and directors, the same cannot be said for appointees to the other legal structures studied. In particular, the case law in this area is confused. Consequently, commentators and regulators alike, in seeking to explain duties to appointees who are not directors or trustees proper, and without knowing what a court would actually decide if the point were ever tested, have assumed that the trustee is the proper analogy to draw. This has led to the development of the 'quasi-trustee', although the term has no recognised legal basis.

Confused terminology

A37 In terms of case law there have been a number of legal judgments in this century and the last which consider the position of appointees to charitable companies and statutory and chartered corporations, and refer to the relevant appointees as being trustees or analogous to trustees.[78] However, these cases do not provide a firm legal foundation for establishing the skill and care duty for such appointees, either because they assume the analogy, without actually hearing argument on the point;[79] or because they are not dealing with the specific question of a duty of skill and care, but with some other point of dispute.[80]

A38 Frequently, questions of how the PSO holds its property are in issue, with the assumption being made that where a PSO is a charity, a trust must be involved.[81] Following the case of *Liverpool & District Hospital for Diseases of the Heart v Attorney General*[82] it is now generally agreed that charitable companies (and by implication, statutory corporations also) do not hold their general property on trust (although they can and do hold it for exclusively charitable purposes[83]). Therefore, neither the PSO nor the appointees are trustees proper.[84] However, Slade J in the *Liverpool Hospital* case held that "the position of the [corporation] in relation to its assets has at all times been analogous to a trustee for charitable purposes".[85]

---

[77] *Re Waterman's Will Trusts v Sutton* [1952] 2 All ER 1054, per Harman J, and *Bartleet v Barclays Bank Trust Co* [1980] Ch 515.

[78] See, for example, *In re the French Protestant Hospital* [1951] Ch 567 (chartered eleemosynary corporation); *Soldiers' Sailors' and Airmen's Families Association v Attorney General* [1968] 1 All ER 448 (chartered corporation); *Re Dominion Students' Hall Trust* [1947] Ch 183 (charitable company limited by guarantee).

[79] In *Re Dominion Students' Hall Trust ibid* the court assumed there was a trust in operation because the company had charitable objects; In *Soldiers' Sailors' and Airmen's Families Association v AG ibid* counsel conceded that the chartered corporation was in the position of a trustee with regard to its funds, so no argument on the point was heard.

[80] In *Re French Protestant Hospital ibid* Danckwerts J held that the appointees were technically not trustees, but assumed that the chartered corporation was a trust, and decided that the appointees were in the same fiduciary position as trustees. The case concerned a proposed amendment to the governing instrument to allow the appointees to award themselves remuneration (for which see the fiduciary duties of appointees, pages 32 ff below), and did not deal with the skill and care duty.

[81] See paragraph 3.34 above for a discussion of trusts and charity property.

[82] [1981] 1 Ch 193. See also *In re Vernon's Will Trusts* [1972] 1 Ch 300, per Buckley J at 303 E–F.

[83] Exempt charities hold their general property for exclusively charitable purposes, e.g. further education colleges, post-1992 universities, grant maintained schools – but this does not create a trust proper.

[84] In the case of chartered corporations which are eleemosynary in nature (see paragraph 3.46 above), the property is, strictly speaking, held on trust by the PSO, but the appointees themselves are still not trustees in the true sense of the word.

[85] [1981] 1 Ch 193 at 214 F–G. This part of the decision concerned the ability of the court to exercise its charitable jurisdiction over the corporation, so as to order a *cy-près* scheme.

A charitable duty of skill and care

A39 Following such case law and prompted by the need to ensure high standards from appointees, regulators have frequently relied upon these analogies to treat their appointees as trustees. The Charity Commission has been at the forefront of advocating these high standards, and has developed a 'charitable duty of skill and care', based upon the trustee standard.[86] This standard is applied to all charity appointees (collectively called 'trustees' in the Commission's guidance) regardless of the legal structure of the PSO.[87] Thus, directors of charitable companies are placed under the higher trustee standard. It should be noted that the guidance produced is not a statement of the law, but a practical guide, setting out the 'charitable duties' of appointees.[88]

A40 Other regulators have also relied upon the trustee standard when producing guidance for appointees. See, for example, the guidance provided by the Further Education Funding Council for further education college governors.[89] The term 'quasi-trustee' has been used by legal commentators also.[90]

A41 While this development cannot be criticised from a practical point of view – it does after all require an appropriately high standard of care from appointees – it raises other problems. For example, a trustee proper enjoys certain forms of protection from liability which are not available to other types of appointee.[91] Yet in the development of the quasi-trustee, it is the *duties* of the appointee which are focused upon, and not the availability of corresponding protection. Therefore, where guidance suggests that appointees are trustees proper, it has the potential to mislead if appointees think they will automatically benefit from the protection afforded to a trustee proper.[92]

A42 Equally, trustees are subject to specific legislative provisions, e.g. the Trustee Investment Act 1961 and the Trustee Act 1925, and, as this study outlines, are afforded different treatment in terms of personal liability to their counterparts in other legal structures. While the quasi-trustee should not be subject to such provisions by analogy, again, there is the potential for misleading guidance to be provided.

A43 While designed to ensure the highest standards of conduct from appointees, there is the potential for the development of the quasi-trustee to leave appointees with the impression that the courts will treat them in all respects as trustees when, in the absence of relevant case law, that is a distinctly questionable assumption.

Analogy with a director

A44 The position of the appointee to industrial and provident societies is also uncertain. Where the society is not a charity,[93] it has been suggested that the duty of skill and care is that of a company

---

[86] See for example Charity Commission Guide CC3 *Responsibilities of Charity Trustees* (March 1996), and the use of the word 'prudent' to describe the skill and care duties.

[87] All of the publications of the Charity Commission contain the following definition: "Trustees means charity trustees. Charity Trustees are the people who, under the charity's governing instrument are responsible for the general control and management of the administration of a charity." This is derived from s.97 of the Charities Act 1993.

[88] The term 'trustee' is used in the Charities Act 1993 to delineate those appointees who fall within the ambit of the act, and the Charity Commission's jurisdiction. It is a wide definition, but it is clear that (a) the term is not being used in the sense of a true trust and (b) that its effect is limited to matters arising out of the Charities Act, and not more generally.

[89] *Guide for College Governors* (May 1994) FEFC.

[90] See, for example, Hyams *The potential liabilities of governors of education institutions* Education and the Law 1994 6 (4) 191.

[91] E.g. section 61 Trustee Act 1925; the question of protection generally is dealt with in Chapter 6.

[92] See, for example, the Further Education Funding Council *Guide for College Governors* (May 1994), paragraphs 6.23 and 11.20.

[93] See Appendix A.

director.[94] However, where societies are charities (albeit exempt ones) it is open to question whether the higher trustee standard would apply, for the above reasons.[95] Therefore, as with the appointees dealt with above, committee members of societies are usually advised to act in accordance with the trustee standard.

Potential liability

A45 The personal liability which arises from the imposition of a duty of skill and care concerns losses which may be caused to the PSO if appointees do not act in accordance with the standards expected of them.

A46 If, through want of the proper exercise of skill, or failure to take the requisite care, the PSO incurs financial loss, the PSO has a right of action for damages against the appointee. The amount of damages will depend upon the nature of the loss attributable to the appointee's conduct. The law on damages is complicated, and there are special rules on the types of loss which are legally attributable to an appointee's breach of duty. It is beyond the scope of this study to discuss such rules, but the clear principle to be applied is that loss which naturally and reasonably arises from the appointee's conduct will form the quantum of the damages.[96]

A47 The identity of the person imbued with the right to sue will vary between the different legal structures. For the corporate structure, the PSO or responsible body's legal personality will have capacity to sue. For the unincorporated association a member (in a representative capacity) may sue, and for the trust, the fellow trustees may bring proceedings.[97]

Law reform proposals

A48 As part of the work on a new legal structure for charities, to replace the trust and the unincorporated association,[98] it has been suggested that the duties and responsibilities of appointees in any new structure could be defined by statute, including the standard of care to be exercised by those controlling the corporation.[99] No published details were available at the time of writing, but the definition of the skill and care duty would need to take account of the issues raised above, and could begin to clarify the confusion that exists in this area.

A49 Equally, the Deakin Report proposed that the present law relating to 'charity trustees' (in the wider sense) should be codified under a new Charity Trustees Act, to bring together in one place the relevant law and set out all the general duties and powers.[100] No further work has been done on this proposal.

Conclusions

A50 Appointees need to ensure that they understand the model against which they will be judged in order to discharge their duty of skill and care. In particular, appointees need to know how much attention they are required to pay to the affairs of the PSO in order to fulfil their duty of care. Professional appointees will bring greater skills with them than the lay appointee, and will be judged by consequently higher standards.

---

[94] See Taussig *Housing Associations and their Committees: A guide to the legal framework* (1992) NFHA, p20. This guide does not take account of the changes effected by the Housing Act 1996, but it remains one of the few legal publications specifically directed at industrial and provident societies and the legal position of their appointees.

[95] Taussig, *ibid,* p22.

[96] See *McGregor on Damages* (16th ed 1997) for details of the rules governing damages for breaches of a common law duty.

[97] There is also a role for third parties here: see Chapter 6 for a discussion of the discretion to bring proceedings vested in the Charity Commission and the Attorney General.

[98] See paragraph A13 above.

[99] This was the conclusion of the joint project, in its first outline proposals.

[100] *Meeting the challenge of change: voluntary action into the 21st century* – The report of the Commission on the Future of the Voluntary Sector, NCVO Publications (1996) paragraphs 3.5.1–3.

A51 For those appointees whose duty of skill and care is defined by analogy with a trustee, rather than by direct case law, there is a need to ensure clarity of advice about the standards which apply to them, and the consequent forms of protection available to them. The imposition of the trustee duty upon appointees who are regarded as 'quasi-trustees' by their regulators or PSO cannot be criticised, since it imposes the highest possible standards upon appointees. However, guidance issued to such appointees should be as clear as possible about the extent of the trustee comparison.

A52 In the longer term, clarification of the standards required of appointees would be beneficial to PSOs and appointees, whether by the courts or by means of legislation.

DUTY THREE: The fiduciary responsibilities

Overview

A53 'Fiduciary responsibilities' are a set of strict legal requirements which, just like the duty of skill and care, define the manner in which an appointee must act towards a PSO.[101] They are based on a concept, developed by the courts under their equitable jurisdiction, that people who are given powers to exercise in the interests of others should have restrictions placed upon how they use those powers. The restrictions are designed to ensure that people act with *loyalty* and *good faith* towards the PSO when performing any task allotted to them.[102]

A54 It is generally agreed that fiduciary responsibilities will attach to relationships as a matter of fact, rather than a matter of law: it has been said that the category of relationships which attract fiduciary duties is not closed.[103] In the case of the legal structures considered in the study, trustees and directors have both been held by the courts to be fiduciaries.[104] While the courts have yet to rule specifically that appointees to the other four structures studied are fiduciaries, the quality and nature of these relationships (involving the provision of powers to be exercised for the benefit of others) is such that it seems improbable that the courts would hold them not to be so if asked to rule on the point.[105]

A55 The attribution of fiduciary responsibilities to all appointees is supported by the fact that such responsibilities are found expressed in many PSOs' governing instruments, and in the regulatory requirements laid down for different legal structures of PSO.

A56 It is interesting to note that six of the seven 'Nolan' principles of public life, developed by the Committee on Standards in Public Life, while not based on any legal study, mirror the content of fiduciary responsibilities developed by the courts over time:

Selflessness
Integrity
Objectivity
Accountability
Openness
Honesty

---

[101] Some legal commentators would class the duty of skill and care as a fiduciary responsibility (see, for example, J Dollimore *Liabilities of Charity Trustees* Charity Law & Practice Review 2 1993/4 (vol 1) 69, at 71). While both take their root from the law of equity, they have been treated distinctly in the study.

[102] Company law extends this definition to include a duty towards employees and shareholders in certain circumstances, but this is not within the scope of this study.

[103] See *Underhill and Hayton Law of Trusts and Trustees* (15th ed 1995) p16.

[104] *Hamilton v Wright* (1842) 9 Cl&F 111; *Aberdeen Ry Co v Blaikie Bros* (1854) 1 Macq 461, at 471; *Regal (Hastings) Ltd v Gulliver* [1967] 2 AC 134n. The third important class of acknowledged fiduciary for the study of PSOs is that of agents and principals (see *Bowstead & Reynolds on Agency* (16th ed 1996), chap 6). In the case of unincorporated associations in particular, executive committee members will often act as agent for the members of the association as a whole, and owe fiduciary obligations accordingly.

[105] There are divergent views on this point, but it is the author's view that a court would impress upon all appointees the duties outlined here, and in Duty Four below. With regard to appointees to statutory corporations being fiduciaries, Megarry VC in *Tito v Waddell* (No 2) [1977] Ch 106 at 228 D–E, held that a duty imposed by statute to perform certain functions did not give rise to fiduciary obligations generally, unless some intention to the contrary appears in the statute. However, the functions under consideration with regard to modern statutory corporations are very different to those under consideration in that case, and it is submitted that the courts are more likely to follow the line taken in *AG v De Winton* [1906] 2 Ch 106, where a borough treasurer (to a municipal (statutory) corporation) was held to be a fiduciary.

A57 Thus there is public acceptance that it is appropriate for appointees to be subject to these duties, as well as a legal requirement.

A58 While the duties which are set out in this section have been termed 'fiduciary responsibilities' in the study, the phrase is not used uniformly in guidance or legal commentary to describe such duties. They may also go under the title 'trust duties'[106] or 'charitable duties'.[107]

The governing instruments

A59 The imposition of fiduciary responsibilities by the law is the main area where the terms of a PSO's governing instruments can affect the precise duty imposed. Appointees can find that the duty placed upon them is specifically enunciated in the governing instruments, or they may find its requirements are tempered, or the duty removed altogether. Where particular PSOs have a common position in this respect, reference is included below. Otherwise, the basic legal position is defined on the assumption that the governing instruments do not affect it.

The responsibilities

A60 There are two specific duties which arise under a fiduciary responsibility which *all appointees* need to be aware of:

  (a) **A duty to act in the interests of the PSO; and**

  (b) **A duty to look after the assets of the PSO.**[108]

A61 They do not have equal force or identical requirements for all the PSOs studied, and each aspect of the duties is described in turn below, by reference to the legal classification developed in Chapter 3.

(a) A duty to act in the interests of the PSO

A62 Except to the extent that the governing instruments of their PSO allow them to do so, appointees:

  (i) must not profit from their position; and

  (ii) must not allow a conflict of interest to arise.[109]

Not profiting from one's position

A63 Appointees' work on a responsible body may provide them with opportunities to receive personal benefit. Examples include being paid for their services or having the responsible body conclude a contract from which they, or those associated with them (family or business) will profit (directly or indirectly). Appointees are under a duty not to make any such personal profit unless the governing instruments (or the court) authorise them so to do.

A64 The governing instruments of many PSOs specifically reiterate this duty and prevent remuneration being paid to appointees, beyond out of pocket expenses. The exceptions in this study are NHS trusts and some NDPBs and registered charities which provide small payments out of PSO funds, but nothing equivalent to a full salary.[110] Remuneration can be given a wide interpretation, so that benefits in kind, hospitality

---

[106] The duties of a true trustee are, properly speaking, a distinct sub-set of the equitable fiduciary duty. The substance of these duties has been analysed below, under the overall heading 'fiduciary responsibilities'.

[107] As discussed at paragraph A39 ff above, appointees to registered charities receive guidance from the Charity Commission on their duties, which are known as 'charitable duties'. Many of these are based upon the fiduciary obligations explained in this chapter.

[108] Classification in this area is particularly difficult. The study deals with two further duties, under the heading 'governance responsibilities' (in Duty Four below), which could be included under the general heading of fiduciary responsibilities. However, for ease of comprehension (and for the reasons set out in the next section), the duties have been distinguished. It should be noted that there is legal overlap between Duties Three and Four as described in the text.

[109] See *Bray v Ford* [1896] AC 44, at 51–52 for Lord Hershell's classic definition of the fiduciary duty of loyalty and disinterest.

[110] See Appendix B for remuneration details, and the policy of the Charity Commission on remuneration clauses in governing instruments for registered charities. The law has recently changed with respect to registered social landlords which are industrial and provident societies, and the ban on paying remuneration to board members has been lifted, although the interim maximum specified by the Housing Corporation is £50 per annum (see Circular R5–37/96 and Version 4 of the Corporation Guidance on payments and benefits).

and even personal liability insurance can be the subject of this rule, if the governing instruments do not allow the specific benefit.[111]

A65 In the case of contracts or other transactions from which an appointee may benefit, the basic rule is that here also appointees must not derive personal profit from any such action, and therefore contracts between appointee and PSO are not allowed.[112] However, in many PSOs procedures are set down in governing instruments by which a proposed benefit can be authorised by the responsible body, and thereby legitimately received by the appointee.[113] This represents an area where the strict fiduciary duties can be tempered by the governing instruments, although the rules normally include the stipulation that the appointee be absent from the responsible body's vote on the matter.

A66 For some legal structures and some types of PSO, legislation also affects the degree to which governing instruments can amend the basic fiduciary responsibility. Thus, company directors are bound by the terms of section 317 of the Companies Act 1985 which requires directors to disclose to the board any interest, direct or indirect, which they may have in a contract, transaction or arrangement with the company;[114] and registered social landlords must abide by the terms of Part 1 of Schedule 1 to the Housing Act 1996, which controls what payments or other benefits can be made to appointees, or members of their families.[115]

A67 This fiduciary responsibility will not prevent appointees from receiving legitimate payment for work they have performed in some capacity for the PSO, other than as an appointee, provided such work has been properly authorised by the responsible body.

No conflict of interest to arise

A68 Appointees should not allow any personal interest to conflict with their duties to the PSO, or put themselves in a position where a conflict could arise.[116] Indeed, appointees must act in the best interests of their PSO, and not for any ulterior or improper purpose.[117] This is another reason for the basic rule forbidding contracts between the appointee and the PSO, described above.

A69 This requirement has particular importance for nominee appointees who retain a primary duty to act in accordance with the best interests of the PSO, and not the particular interests of the constituency which has elected them, or the party nominating them.[118] This means, in practice, that nominee appointees must exercise their own judgement in a matter, and not blindly follow instructions from their nominator.

A70 The governing instruments of many PSOs will require a register of interests to be maintained to support this duty, and, in the case of TECs, the government licence imposes requirements, in addition to the company law rules, to ensure that the directors act as individuals and not as representatives of other organisations.[119]

---

[111] See Chapter 6, paragraphs 6.69 ff for further details of personal liability insurance.

[112] See, for example, *Albion Steel & Wire Co v Martin* [1875] 1 Ch D 580, at 585.

[113] See, for example, the standard Instrument of Government for Further Education Colleges, paragraph 10 (SI 1992/1963).

[114] Directors are also restricted from contracting under certain specified types of contract with the company, e.g. service contracts or loan contracts – see *Palmer's Company Law* (looseleaf work) vol 2 paras 8.520–8.530.

[115] Replacing section 15 of the Housing Associations Act 1985, and see footnote 110 above.

[116] The cases enunciating these rules are mainly concerned with companies, see, for example, *North-West Transportation Co v Beatty* (1887) 12 App Cas 589; *Transvaal Lands Co v New Belgium Land and Development Co* [1914] 2 Ch 485.

[117] The rules on acting for a proper purpose have been developed in the context of the fiduciary duties of directors. See *Gower's Principles of Modern Company Law* Davies (6th ed 1997) p 605.

[118] See Denning LJ *Boulting v Association of Cinematograph etc* [1963] 2 QB 606, at 626.

[119] See Appendix A.

(b) A duty to look after the assets of the PSO

A71 Appointees:

> (i) must not misappropriate or misuse the assets of the PSO; and
>
> (ii) must not misuse the information or opportunities of the PSO.[120]

Misappropriation or misuse of assets

A72 This duty appears, at first sight, to be similar to the requirement that appointees must not personally profit from their position, but, in fact, it goes wider than this, because it concerns protection, and in some cases enhancement, of the PSO's assets more generally.

A73 The assets of the PSO must only be applied for the purposes set out in the governing instruments (i.e. the specified public benefit), and appointees have a duty to ensure this happens. No matter how meritorious the use of the assets of the PSO, if it is not a use permitted by the governing instruments, it is a misuse in the eyes of the law.[121]

A74 Accordingly, it is not just personal gain to the appointee which is forbidden, but any improper use of the assets for which appointees are responsible.[122]

A75 Improper use most frequently arises in the context of theft or fraud, and this study does not consider the general law on such criminal conduct.[123] In addition, the legislation regulating companies and industrial and provident societies provides specific offences concerning the misuse or misappropriation of assets.[124]

A76 For trustees, this duty may be somewhat higher than for other appointees, since misuse may include failing to secure the best return on the assets of the trust. Because of the need to be prudent, in order to discharge their skill and care duty trustees must ensure that they do not dissipate or fail to invest the trust property.[125]

A77 This duty does not extend to ensuring that others do not misappropriate or misuse assets. However, it should be noted that it is part of an appointee's skill and care duties to exercise reasonable oversight of co-appointees and agents, for which see Duty Five below on the responsibility of appointees for the acts of others.

Misuse of information or opportunities

A78 This part of an appointee's fiduciary duties has been developed in the context of companies and trusts. Under it appointees have a duty not to use the PSO's assets or information to generate and use a business opportunity from which they will benefit. The duty continues to apply even if the PSO will not be deprived of the chance to exploit the opportunity itself; and where directors acted in good faith and intended the profits of their activity to benefit the company they were still held to have breached this fiduciary duty.[126]

A79 The courts have not considered this aspect of the fiduciary responsibility in the context of a PSO as such, and it is unclear to what extent not-for-profit

---

120 These two duties are often referred to as the 'secret profit' rule.

121 This duty is often ascribed to bodies which apply their property for exclusively charitable purposes, and so it is seen as a 'charitable duty'. In fact, the duty holds good for any PSO, where the governing instruments define a purpose for the use of the organisation's assets (as far as a duty owed to the PSO is concerned). In the commercial context, see for example *Bishopsgate Investment v Maxwell* [1993] BCC 120 Hoffmann LJ at 140 C, G–H.

122 This duty is linked with the governance responsibility of abiding by the terms of the governing instruments generally – see paragraph A122 ff below.

123 But see below, Chapter 5, for the offence of wrongful trading in the context of an insolvent PSO.

124 See s.64 Industrial and Provident Societies Act 1965 creating an offence of misappropriation of a society's assets; and s.212 Insolvency Act 1986 allowing misfeasance proceedings to be taken by a liquidator in insolvency situations where a director has unlawfully received company assets.

125 See Picarda *The Law and Practice Relating to Charities* (2nd ed 1995) p464.

126 See *Regal Hastings Ltd v Gulliver* [1942] 1 All ER 378; [1967] 2 AC 134n (directors breached fiduciary duty even though intended to benefit company not themselves) and *Boardman v Phipps* [1967] 2 AC 46 (trustees legally liable to account for profits made from information which trust could not legally exploit). These were examples where the court was able to exercise its discretion as to the penalty imposed: see Chapter 6 below.

organisations will have information which can be misused in the manner described. Given the growing 'contract culture' in which many PSOs operate however, it is an aspect of the fiduciary duty of which appointees should be aware.

Potential liability

A80 In principle, where appointees fail to abide by any part of the fiduciary responsibilities outlined above, they will become liable to repay any sums they have received without proper authority. This will be the case no matter how well intentioned or innocent the receipt of the payment.

A81 Equally, appointees will have to account for any profits made under transactions or contracts with the PSO which breach the above duty, and from which they benefit.[127]

A82 In terms of misuse of information and opportunities the courts have held that the act of using the particular opportunity personally can be sufficient to breach this duty, and it does not depend on whether or not the profit would or could have gone to the company, whether the appointees acted for the benefit of the company or whether the company suffered or benefited by the action. Where potential liability does arise in these circumstances, protection from the liability actually occurring may well be available.

A83 The law on bringing an action for breach of these duties can be complicated, and is beyond the scope of this study.[128] It will suffice to mention that appointees may well become 'constructive trustees' of any property or money they receive in breach of this duty, creating proprietary rights, as well as personal rights.[129] This distinction will be important to a PSO endeavouring to recover the sums, but does not affect the basic liability of the appointee.

A84 Of the statutory provisions described above, the penalties for failure to comply with these will be fines, in addition to the return of misappropriated property, where appropriate. See also the discussion on disqualification from office in Section C below.

Conclusions

A85 Fiduciary responsibilities impose strict and exacting standards upon appointees. To ensure that they comply with these standards, appointees must understand the terms of the governing instruments of their PSO. In particular, they must understand what personal benefit they may derive from their appointment, and what permitted uses may be made of the PSO's funds. There is considerable guidance for appointees in this area, produced by regulators and PSOs, and it is increasingly difficult for appointees to fail to meet their fiduciary duties except through deliberate wrongdoing.

A86 However, in some, albeit rare, cases potential personal liability can arise where there has been no intentional wrongdoing on the part of appointees. In such cases protection from liability may be available, depending on the legal structure of the PSO (for which see Chapter 6). Further minimising the potential for personal liability from unintentional failure depends on appointees asking for and receiving comprehensive guidance in accordance with the law set out in this chapter.

DUTY FOUR: The governance responsibilities

Overview

A87 As with the fiduciary responsibilities, 'governance responsibilities' regulate how appointees exercise their stewardship of the PSO. They too concern *good faith* and *loyalty* as described above, but they

---

[127] A liability to account is a particular type of remedy available in circumstances of misappropriation.

[128] See any of the standard works on trusts, for example *Underhill and Hayton Law of Trusts and Trustees* (15th ed 1995) chap 7, or *Parker and Mellows The Modern Law of Trusts* (6th ed 1994), chap 8.

[129] Proprietary rights can be more effective when seeking the return of assets from a third party than a merely personal right.

may be regarded as more technical than the requirements outlined in Duty Three, and for this reason they have been distinguished as a duty. Governance responsibilities require appointees to understand the nature of the powers conferred upon them, how they may be exercised, and the limitations on the legal capacity of their responsible body and PSO.

A88   The two aspects of this responsibility are:

   (a) **A duty to act with proper authority; and**
   (b) **A duty to ensure the PSO acts within its governing instruments.**

A89   It is particularly important for appointees to understand this aspect of their duties, since failure to do so can give rise to what is often called a 'technical breach' of duty. This is where an appointee has not been guilty of any culpable behaviour, indeed they may have acted in good faith throughout, but the law imposes a potential liability because the appointee has nonetheless failed to discharge the technical terms of their governance responsibility.

A90   This section describes the two aspects of this responsibility, and the potential liability which can arise.[130] It shows how the legal structure of the PSO can produce different consequences for the personal liability of appointees, particularly in the various corporate structures.

(a)   Acting with proper authority

A91   Appointees must ensure that where they act on behalf of the PSO they have proper authority so to do. This has three aspects to it: achieving a quorum, voting and delegation.

Achieving a quorum

A92   Generally, a responsible body will be required to act collectively when conducting the PSO's business and when taking any decisions. The responsible body for all PSOs will have rules about the minimum number of appointees who need to be present at a meeting in order for the meeting to be quorate, and a decision to be validly made. The entire membership of the responsible body need not necessarily be present, and it will be for the governing instruments to specify the requisite numbers.[131]

Voting

A93   Provided a meeting is quorate, it is not necessary for a decision to be carried unanimously in order for it to be valid. Again, governing instruments will usually indicate whether the majority can bind the minority, and who has a casting vote in the event of equal votes.

A94   The ability of the majority to bind the minority holds good for charity trustees, even if the governing instruments do not indicate that this is the case, which is an exception to the normal rule for trusts.[132]

A95   To avoid administrative complications the law also provides for specified appointees to sign and execute documents on behalf of the responsible body as a whole. Any registered charity (trust, charitable company or unincorporated association) can have documents executed by two of their number.[133] Under the Corporate Bodies' Contracts Act 1960, any corporate structure (except a company) can execute documents by signature of an authorised individual, without the need for the company seal.[134] Equally, the Companies Act 1985 effects similar provisions for companies with regard to documents which would, under the common law, have to be concluded under seal.[135]

---

[130]   This is a subject which merits an entire study of its own. Accordingly, the discussion which follows has been abbreviated, and references are given to relevant legal texts for more detailed discussion.

[131]   In the case of industrial and provident societies the rules need not provide for a quorum, in which case two members are sufficient: *Halsbury's Laws of England* vol 24 (4th ed reissue) para 84.

[132]   See *Re Whiteley* [1910] 1 Ch 600 for the charitable trustee exception.

[133]   S.82 Charities Act 1993.

[134]   S.1.

[135]   S.36A (4).

Delegation

A96 The most important aspect of the duty to act with proper authority, in terms of personal liability, is the question of delegation. Appointees to a responsible body do not have an inherent power to delegate their powers and duties to other people, including other appointees.[136] Therefore, any delegation of a task to an individual appointee or a third party must be specifically authorised by the responsible body, who in turn must have the necessary powers under the PSO's governing instruments, and/or the general law.[137] Usually, specific restrictions are placed on what matters can be delegated by the responsible body, and appointees must usually act collectively when taking decisions.

A97 A distinction is often drawn between tasks involving the use of a discretion (e.g. whether to make an investment), which tend to be non-delegable under governing instruments, and tasks which are of a more administrative nature, which are more likely to be delegable.

A98 It is difficult to generalise further about this aspect of the governance responsibilities, since every PSO will have its own particular rules. The potential liability which can arise from delegating matters to *a third party* is dealt with separately in Duty Five below. The potential liability discussed under this duty is that of *appointees* who agree to act individually on behalf of their responsible body.

Potential liability

A99 If decisions are taken without the responsible body being quorate the resultant decision is void, since it is not a valid act of the responsible body.[138] The particular liability that could arise for the individual appointee in this situation is discussed in paragraphs A122 to A136 below, in the context of abiding by the governing instruments more generally.[139]

A100 The potential consequences for an appointee acting without the proper delegated authority differ noticeably between the different legal structures. In discussing them, a distinction needs to be drawn between a case where the responsible body attempts to delegate a matter to an individual appointee, but it does not, at law, have the power so to do (Case 1), and a case where appointees, acting on their own initiative, believe they have had a power delegated to them, but in fact the responsible body has taken no such decision (Case 2).[140]

Non-corporate structures

A101 For non-corporate structures, appointees can suffer similar consequences in Case 1 and Case 2, and the two may conveniently be dealt with together.

A102 As discussed already, appointees to trusts and unincorporated associations are acting in place of their PSO, so that they already assume a potential personal liability for transactions into which they

---

[136] This duty has, like the fiduciary responsibilities, been developed in the context of trusts and companies (see, for example, *Re County Palatine Loan Co* (1874) 9 Ch App 691 and the cases cited by *Underhill & Hayton Law of Trusts and Trustees* (15th ed 1995) p 618, fn 13,14), but is applicable to all legal structures.

[137] Most legal structures will rely upon powers of delegation from their governing instruments, but trustees enjoy statutory powers of delegation under, inter alia, section 23 of the Trustee Act 1925, irrespective of any powers in the trust deed; and see the Law Commission Consultation Paper No 146 *Trustees' Powers and Duties* (April 1997) for a discussion of the extent to which a trustee's powers to delegate should be reformed.

[138] There are company law cases (decided pre the Company Act reforms referred to below) which have allowed a decision to stand, notwithstanding the want of authority (see the discussion in *Pennington's Company Law* (7th ed 1995) pp 111–117). Any case will depend upon its facts, but it remains the principle that the transaction is void.

[139] The study does not deal with the possibility of obtaining an injunction to restrain acts which have been improperly delegated. It should be noted, however, that such relief will usually be available to members of corporate bodies and unincorporated associations, or representatives of the public interest in charitable trusts, to prevent the proposed conduct taking place.

[140] In this case, the responsible body would have had the power to delegate the matter.

enter to achieve the PSO's ends. However, it is still important for appointees in these structures to ensure that, where they act individually, they have the authority of their responsible body to undertake activities on behalf of the PSO. This is because failure to do so can deprive appointees of certain rights of indemnity from the PSO's funds which would otherwise protect them from actually incurring the liability.[141]

Corporate structures

A103 In PSOs with corporate structures, acting without authority as set out in Case 1 and Case 2 can produce potential liabilities to the PSO itself. Further, in certain circumstances liabilities can arise to third parties under a cause of action known as 'breach of warranty of authority'.

Case 1

The responsible body attempts to delegate a matter to an individual appointee, but it does not, at law, have the power so to do:

A104 Where an appointee in any type of corporate structure acts without authority because the responsible body could not legally delegate the matter to the appointee (although it tried to), a liability can, in principle, arise to the PSO to make good any loss which arises from the unauthorised act. However, in industrial and provident societies and statutory corporations the consequences of the appointee's unauthorised act may well not give rise to any loss. It will be a question of fact in every case, but the general rule is that the act

undertaken by these appointees will be invalid as far as the PSO is concerned because it is undertaken without the necessary power.

A105 If the appointee's conduct in these circumstances cannot commit the PSO to any binding course of action, it is unlikely to have caused any loss to the PSO. In the rare circumstance that it does suffer loss, the PSO could bring an action against the appointee to compensate it for the loss.[142]

A106 While industrial and provident societies and statutory corporations may not be bound by the appointee's conduct, there remains the question of whether the appointee becomes personally liable on the particular transaction (i.e. will be held to have entered into the contract in their own capacity because the PSO could not do so). Such personal liability will not arise unless it can be shown that the appointee intended to undertake the act in question in their personal capacity. Usually, it will be clear from the facts that the appointee was purporting to act on behalf of the PSO, and, therefore, a court is likely to rule that the decision or transaction was not made in an appointee's personal capacity.

A107 The situation is somewhat different for directors of companies and charitable companies. By virtue of the Companies Act 1985,[143] the failure of the responsible body properly to authorise the director because of a lack of power does not invalidate the director's acts as far as anyone dealing with the director in good faith is concerned.[144] The position for charitable companies is similar.[145] Thus, the company can be bound by the particular transaction and may suffer loss directly as a result

---

[141] *Re Johnson* (1880) 15 Ch D 548; *Re Oxley* [1914] 1 Ch 604. See Chapter 6, paragraph 6.99 ff below for a full discussion on this.

[142] But the appointees (of whom the individual appointee is likely to be one) authorising the invalid delegation would also be implicated in the conduct, since they will have breached their own duty to abide by the governing instruments (see paragraph A122 ff below). They will therefore also be liable.

[143] See section 35A, as substituted by the Companies Act 1989.

[144] See *Palmer's Company Law* (looseleaf) vol 1 para 3.304 for details of the statutory definition of 'good faith', but note it is not bad faith even if the other party knows that the act is beyond the powers laid down in the governing instruments (S.35A(2)).

[145] Charitable companies are subject to the same provisions outlined in footnote 144 above, but the Charities Act 1993 alters the test for the third party from a person acting in good faith to a person who gives full consideration for money or money's worth, and who did not know that the act was beyond the power of the directors, or who did not know that the company was a charity; s.65. Thus additional protection is afforded to the charity in these circumstances.

of the appointee's conduct, notwithstanding the want of power on the part of the PSO. In these circumstances, the company retains a right of action against the director personally, which may be worth pursuing if a tangible loss has accrued to the PSO.[146] If the responsible body is involved in the failure to delegate properly, the risk of such action is remote, given the discussion of ratification in Chapter 6 below.

A108 Likewise, appointees to chartered corporations will find that even if their acts have been improperly delegated to them because the PSO lacks the appropriate power in the governing instruments, the acts are good against third parties, but leave the appointee liable to an action from the PSO itself.[147]

A109 Acting without authority in the manner described in Case 1 can also create a potential liability to *third parties* if the appointee's conduct has lead to a purported transaction failing because the PSO itself is not bound; appointees to industrial and provident societies and statutory corporations (but not chartered corporations or companies) can be held responsible for their failure to have proper authority when a third party suffers loss as a result, under what is known as a 'breach of warranty of authority' claim.

A110 This is a right afforded to people who purport to enter into legal relations on the basis of a representation that someone has authority to act for another, but then discover that no such authority existed, and therefore the transaction fails.[148] Thus, the cause of action will arise where the unauthorised act of the appointee involves an agreement with or promise to another person. Liability does not depend on an act of bad faith by the appointee in holding out that they have authority, although the courts have held that where the failure to have authority is a mistake of law (rather than a mistake of fact) no liability arises.

A111 For example, a mistake of fact might be that the responsible body had voted to delegate the matter to the appointee, whereas, in fact, they had not (for which, see Case 2 below); a mistake of law might be that the responsible body had the power to delegate the matter in the first place. In theory therefore, this provides assistance to appointees who act without authority where they have misunderstood their legal position. However, it is not always an easy distinction to draw, and should not be relied upon in the absence of a further case testing the point.[149]

A112 The loss which the third party will be suing for is the failure of the transaction which they thought they were undertaking with the PSO.[150] Because of this, it has been suggested that an action for breach of warranty of authority will not succeed against an appointee if despite not having personal authority, the PSO itself could not have entered into the particular transaction because it was not authorised by its governing instruments to carry out the particular act.[151] In this circumstance the third party would be left without any redress at law.[152]

---

[146] See s.35A (5) *ibid*, preserving the common law rights of the company against the director; however, see also the role of ratification in Chapter 6 post.

[147] For the reasons set out at paragraph A136 below.

[148] *Collen v Wright* (1857) 7 E & B 301, affd (1857) 8 E & B 647; *Yonge v Toynbee* [1910] 1 KB 215. For a detailed exposition of this type of claim see *Bowstead & Reynolds on Agency* 16th ed (1996) at chap 9, art 107. The warranty may relate to actions other than those resulting in a contract – para 9-061.

[149] See *Bowstead & Reynolds op cit* at para 9-063.

[150] In terms of a measure of damages *Bowstead & Reynolds op cit* states that where a contract fails to materialise due to the lack of authority, the loss is "prima facie the amount of damages that could have been recovered from [the PSO] in an action if [the PSO] had duly authorised and subsequently refused to perform the contract, together with the costs and expenses … of any legal proceedings", at para 9-071.

[151] I.e. it is not the power to delegate which is lacking, but the primary power to do the act which is to be delegated.

[152] See *Bowstead & Reynolds op cit* at paragraph 9-062, and the commentary of Hyams in *Higher and further education dismissals – problem areas and their consequences for corporations and governors* Education and the Law 8 (2) 1996, at pp 148–9. Even if liability could arise if the PSO had no power to carry out the act, as *Bowstead & Reynolds* points out, the loss is likely to be nil, under the principle described at footnote 150 (at para 9-074).

A113 The situation is very different for third parties dealing *bona fide* with directors of companies, since, as mentioned above, the acts of directors in these circumstances are automatically validated by the law and are binding on the PSO in most circumstances.[153] Likewise, the transaction will take effect if the PSO is a chartered corporation. Since such transactions will be valid as far as the third party is concerned, there is no basis for a breach of warranty of authority claim to be advanced. Of course, in the event that the contract is not entered into *bona fide* by the third party as required by the Companies Act 1985 it will be void, and an action for breach of warranty of authority will arise, as described for the other types of corporate structure.

Case 2

Appointees act on their own initiative in the belief that they have had a power delegated to them, but in fact the responsible body has taken no such decision:

A114 As with Case 1, the treatment of appointees under Case 2 varies according to the legal structure of the PSO. However, different rules apply in a Case 2 situation which is why the two scenarios need to be distinguished.

A115 For industrial and provident societies and statutory corporations the consequences of the appointees' unauthorised conduct will not be to automatically render the results of the conduct invalid as far as the PSO is concerned, as was the position in Case 1. This is because in this case the PSO does have the power to authorise the appointee's conduct, and the difficulty is one of the extent of the actual authority delegated. While the appointee may have had no actual authority, it is possible for the law to imply that there was apparent authority. Apparent authority will arise if representations were made by the responsible body giving the impression that authority had been conferred.[154]

If such apparent authority is established then, in contrast to Case 1, the transaction could be valid, and binding upon the PSO.

A116 In this case there could be a loss to the PSO as a result of the appointee's unauthorised conduct, and the PSO's right of action against the individual appointee could be invoked. However, there will be no liability to third parties under a breach of warranty of authority claim if the PSO is bound by the appointee's conduct, since third parties will have suffered no harm by the lack of authority.

A117 As far as companies are concerned under Case 2, it is possible for liability to third parties to arise in a way that is not possible under Case 1. This is because the protection afforded by the Companies Act 1985 discussed above only covers acts of the individual director which are authorised, or purportedly authorised by the responsible body. Thus, if the appointee acts without even a purported authorisation (and there is no possibility of asserting the doctrine of apparent authority[155]), the PSO company would not automatically be bound by the transaction.

A118 Therefore, directors could find themselves in the same position as appointees to the other corporate structures, and potentially liable for a breach of warranty of authority claim from a third party whose transaction is ineffective as far as the PSO is concerned.

A119 Appointees in chartered corporations are probably in a similar position to company directors under Case 2, although there is little authority on the point.

A120 Clearly, much depends on the facts of any particular case as to why no delegated authority has been granted, but the principles set out in the two cases establish the potential legal basis for personal liability to arise for appointees.

---

[153] See footnotes 143 and 145 above.

[154] A discussion of the law on apparent and pretended authority is beyond the scope of this study. Readers are referred to *Bowstead & Reynolds op cit* Chapter 8, Art 74 *et seq*.

[155] It has been held that ordinary non-executive directors are not generally invested with any apparent authority to act on the company's behalf: *George Whitechurch Ltd v Cavanagh* [1902] AC 117.

A121 Moreover, both cases illustrate how appointees could be potentially liable for a technical breach of their governance duties. There may be no intentional wrongdoing on their part, but if their conduct and the delegation are unauthorised then appointees can expose themselves to the types of claim discussed above.

(b) Ensuring the PSO acts within its governing instruments

A122 The second aspect of appointees' governance responsibilities is to ensure that the PSO acts within its governing instruments. The governing instruments of all legal structures specify powers, duties and purposes which regulate the activities of the PSO. All appointees are under a duty to ensure that such requirements are complied with.

A123 The general law can supplement the terms of governing instruments, in particular by supplying additional powers which are automatically afforded to appointees.[156] However, any express terms in the governing instruments must be consulted and followed by appointees.

A124 This duty is linked with Duty Three concerning the duty to look after the PSO's assets, since any expenditure sanctioned by appointees upon matters not authorised by the governing instruments is also a breach of their fiduciary responsibilities.[157] Therefore, there is overlap between these two duties.

Potential liability

A125 As with the liability for unauthorised acts of appointees, discussed above, the consequences of failing to comply with this aspect of the

governance responsibilities differ between the different legal structures.

A126 If appointees commit their PSO to a course of action which is not permitted by the governing instruments, the potential for personal liability will arise both to the PSO and to third parties, depending on the legal structure of the PSO, and the nature of the particular conduct. This is discussed below for corporate and non-corporate structures.

Corporate structures

A127 In providing a legal personality to a PSO with a corporate structure, the governing instruments will set out the 'objects' which the PSO can achieve (i.e. the particular public benefit it is to provide) and the 'powers' which the responsible body can exercise (i.e. to enter into contracts, purchase land, employ staff, invest surplus assets).

A128 The objects are particulary important since they define the capacity of the PSO's legal personality; as explained in Chapter 3, statutory corporations, industrial and provident societies and companies can only do those things which they are specifically authorised to do (or which are clearly ancillary to their purposes). Further, in achieving these objects the responsible body may only exercise the powers awarded to it in the governing instruments (subject to any powers afforded by the general law).

A129 The importance of these terms is that they define the capacity of the PSO to commit valid and binding acts. Using legal terminology, acts which are outside a PSO's objects are *ultra vires*[158] and it is the duty of appointees to ensure that such *ultra vires* acts are not committed by the responsible body.[159]

---

[156] See, for example, the powers of company directors under the Companies Act 1985, and the powers of trustees under the Trustee Act 1925; and for appointees of registered charities, the Charities Act 1993.

[157] Paragraph A71 above.

[158] In the context of companies the term *ultra vires* has been used to cover two types of conduct: acts which are outside the capacity of the company; and acts which are within its capacity, but outside the authority of the directors (see *Rolled Steel Ltd v BSC* [1986] 1 Ch 246, 287). The term is used in the first sense in the study. The second sense is covered by the discussion on delegation under Case 2 above.

[159] One commentator has suggested that the duty not to cause a statutory corporation to act *ultra vires* is not in itself a free-standing duty, but is only imposed where there is some other fiduciary duty (see Hyams *Higher and further education dismissals – problem areas and their consequences for corporations and governors* Education and the Law 8 (2) 1996). As explained at paragraph A54 above, it is considered probable that a fiduciary duty would be imposed by a court on appointees to statutory PSOs, and this aspect of the governance duties is likely to be an important part of the duty.

Equally appointees must ensure that they have the powers to carry out any activity.

A130 For some PSOs any act which is not authorised by its governing instruments will be invalid and void (e.g. statutory corporations and industrial and provident societies);[160] for others, such acts may take effect as far as third parties are concerned, but are still improper as far as the PSO is concerned (e.g. companies).[161]

A131 Chartered corporations are in a slightly different position, since they have the capacity of a natural person, notwithstanding their corporate status. Thus the law treats them as legally capable of doing anything, regardless of any objects specified in the charter.[162] However, see also the discussion of charitable purposes below.

A132 As with the unauthorised acts of appointees described above, the personal liability which may arise from an *ultra vires* act depends upon the legal structure of the PSO.

A133 For companies, the Companies Act 1985 renders acts of the PSO which are outside its objects or outwith the powers of the directors, valid as far as third parties are concerned.[163] As was the position under Case 1 above, the PSO retains a right of action against individual directors if they are responsible for the act which is outside the company's objects and the PSO suffers a loss as a result of being bound by the action.

A134 For industrial and provident societies and statutory corporations, acts which are *ultra vires* will be void and unenforceable as far as the PSO is concerned i.e. a contract which is outside the capacity of the

PSO will not bind the PSO. A potential action by the PSO against the appointee would exist, if any loss could be demonstrated in these circumstances, but as with the position of appointees under Case 1 above, such loss is unlikely.

A135 It is also possible that a claim for misrepresentation could be pursued by a third party against an appointee in an industrial and provident society or statutory corporation in these circumstances, if it could be shown that the appointee made a specific representation as to the capacity or the powers of the PSO. Unlike the situation in Case 1 above, where there is an implied warranty that the appointee has the authority of the PSO, there is no implied warranty as to the capacity of the PSO. However, in the absence of specific and express words by the appointee, it is unlikely that any such claim would succeed. In these circumstances, the third party may proceed against the PSO for a *quantum meruit*[164] of any work performed for the PSO under the void transaction, or a restitutionary award. It will be a question of fact in every case whether this will give rise to some liability which the PSO can attempt to recover from the individual appointee, under its rights described in paragraph A134.

A136 Chartered corporations are in a similar situation to companies in terms of the consequences of acting *ultra vires*, although the legal basis for their position is not statute law, but the charter itself. As stated earlier, chartered corporations have a complete legal personality and may act as a natural person does. Therefore, as far as third parties are concerned, acts performed which are unauthorised by the governing instruments nonetheless bind the PSO, and are good against

---

[160] For recent case law on *ultra vires* invalidity in statutory corporations see *Hazell v Hammersmith and Fulham LBC* [1992] 2 AC 1, and *Credit Suisse v Allerdale BC* [1996] 3 WLR 894. See also Appendix E below on the use of indemnities for local authority nominee appointees.

[161] Thereby entitling the PSO to take action against the individual director for the conduct.

[162] See *Sutton's Hospital Case* (1612) 10 Co Rep; *Baroness Wenlock v River Dee Co* (1883) 36 Ch 675n at 685; *British South Africa Co v De Beers Ltd* [1910] 1 Ch 354.

[163] S.35 – re: objects and s.35A re: powers. In the case of the latter, the third party must be acting bona fide, as described earlier. The additional requirements for charitable companies set out in footnote 145 apply here also. For a detailed discussion of this complex area and its history see *Pennington's Company Law* (7th ed 1995) p111 ff. Note also the question of acting for an improper purpose discussed under fiduciary responsibilities at paragraph A68 above.

[164] A remedy available to a party who has performed works or services under a contract that is later held void. The party is entitled to the value of the works or services performed in reliance on the terms of the contract, notwithstanding that it is void.

the outside world.[165] Accordingly there is no potential for a breach of warranty of authority claim. However, if the acts concerned contravene the domestic statutes of the chartered corporation then the responsible appointees could be liable to the extent that the PSO suffers loss as a result.[166]

Non-corporate structures

A137 The concepts of legal capacity, and acting *ultra vires* as described above are not applicable to non-corporate structures because they have no legal personality. However, this does not mean that appointees are free to do what they wish in relation to the PSO.

A138 For appointees to unincorporated associations, the purposes of the association and the powers of the committee will be laid down in the rules of the association. These rules form a contract between all of the members. There is no question of lack of capacity rendering the acts of the committee members void as far as third parties are concerned (since the appointee will be acting in place of the PSO).[167] However, as between the members of the association, appointees are under a duty to use the assets of the association only for purposes set out in the rules and to exercise powers as defined in the rules.[168]

A139 Similarly a trust deed will specify the purposes upon which the trust funds are to be expended, and the means which can be employed by the trustees in execution of the trust. These are the directions of the creator of the trust. It is the duty of trustees to ensure both are followed.[169] As with

unincorporated associations, the acts of trustees in breach of the governing instruments are not rendered void as far as third parties are concerned, but it is a breach of duty to fail to abide by the terms of the governing instruments.

A140 The law on personal liability for appointees to non-corporate structures for failure to observe the governing instruments is similar to the position outlined for their unauthorised acts, as set out in paragraph A101 above. Where an improper use of the assets of the PSO is involved, the position will be as set out in paragraphs A72 to A77 above.

Charitable purposes

A141 In addition to the limitations described above, PSOs which are registered or exempt charities are bound by law to apply their funds for exclusively charitable purposes (as defined in the governing instruments). Failure to do so risks depriving the PSO of its charitable status,[170] as well as having the potential to amount to a breach of the duty to abide by the governing instruments.

Injunctions

A142 For registered charities, where it is proposed to enter into a contract made outside the charity's purposes (i.e. non-charitable or other charitable purposes, however beneficial), the courts may restrain the activities by injunction at the request of the Attorney General.[171] For companies the right of members to obtain an injunction is also retained, although it is limited.[172]

---

[165] See the judgment of Browne-Wilkinson V-C on behalf of the visitor in *Pearce v University of Aston (No 2)* [1991] 2 All ER 469 at 475 F.

[166] It is debateable whether such liability would fall to the corporation's visitor to determine or the courts. See paragraph C9 ff below for a discussion of visitation. While claims of this type may involve interpretation of the internal laws, which is within the exclusive jurisdiction of the visitor, the fact that many chartered corporations will be eleemosynary institutions, holding their property on trust, means that the court may be the proper forum if the dispute involves allegations of a breach of the terms of the trust.

[167] See Duty One above.

[168] *Baker v Jones* [1954] 1 WLR 806; *Taylor v NUM* [1985] BCLC 237.

[169] See *Underhill & Hayton Law of Trusts and Trustees* (15th ed 1995) p468; and Picarda *The Law and Practice Relating to Charities* (2nd ed 1995) pp 460, 479.

[170] See Picarda, *op cit*, at p460.

[171] See *A-G v Ross* [1985] 3 All ER 334.

[172] See ss 35(2), 35A of the Companies Act 1985.

Conclusions

A143 As with the fiduciary responsibilities, the governance responsibilities impose strict requirements on appointees that they comply with the terms of the PSO's governing instruments. Appointees must ensure that they act with proper authority and that their acts or decisions are within the capacity of the PSO at all times, whether they serve corporate or non-corporate structures. Provision of guidance and information in this area is particularly important, since there is considerable scope for 'technical breach' to occur if appointees do not understand the limits on their powers. Furthermore, liability can arise to third parties, as well as to the PSO.

A144 With the benefit of proper information on the subject it will be rare for personal liability to arise save in cases where appointees have acted in bad faith. However, failure to act in accordance with the governing instruments can, in very limited circumstances, give rise to personal liability without wrongdoing on the part of the appointee, e.g. in breach of warranty of authority cases.

A145 The particular legislative protection afforded to directors of companies when exercising their governance responsibilities comes from a perceived need to achieve fairness for third parties dealing with companies, rather than a wish to afford additional protection to the appointees themselves.[173] Hence, directors receive greater protection from third party claims than other appointees in corporate structures, but are consequently more vulnerable to an action from the PSO itself because their unauthorised acts can bind the company.[174] At present only company directors are subject to these *ultra vires* rules, although appointees in chartered corporations benefit in a similar way, for different reasons.

DUTY FIVE: Responsibility for the acts of others

Overview

A146 So far the discussion of responsibilities owed to the PSO has focused on the conduct of appointees themselves. This section deals with the question of appointees' responsibilities for the acts of staff and agents engaged by a PSO. Two situations need to be considered:

    (a) where someone under the employment or direction of the PSO wrongfully causes loss to the PSO, e.g. by misappropriating funds; and

    (b) where someone under the employment or direction of the PSO injures a third party, e.g. libels them, or causes personal injury to them.[175]

A147 Appointees' personal liability for either type of conduct depends on whether the PSO has a corporate or non-corporate structure and whether the other person is an agent or an employee of the PSO.

Agents v employees

A148 An agent is someone who has the authority to act on behalf of somebody else (the principal) and thereby affect the principal's legal relations with third parties. Such authority may result from a contract, or it may arise by implication of law, or from the facts of the relationship. An employee is someone who is contractually engaged to work for somebody else (the employer) and carry out their requirements.[176] The essential difference between the two is that the former has power to act as if they were the principal (to the extent of their authority) whereas the latter is employed to

---

[173] The statutory provisions were introduced to conform with the First Company Law Directive (68/151 EEC) requiring equality of protection for third parties dealing with companies.

[174] Although see Chapter 6 below for the various methods a company can use to sanction retrospectively the acts of its errant director, by ratification.

[175] For details of the legal basis for these tortious acts see paragraphs B7 ff below.

[176] An employee is distinguished from an independent contractor by the terms of the contract of employment which will make the employee the servant of the employer.

undertake tasks for the employer, but does not, as a matter of general law, have authority to act in place of the employer, so as to alter the other's legal position.[177]

A149 PSOs may use both agents and employees in carrying out their work. As will be appreciated from the discussion in Chapter 3, non-corporate PSOs cannot fulfil the role of principal or employer as a matter of law, because they have no legal personality. Accordingly, appointees themselves must occupy such positions (individually or collectively). On the other hand, corporate PSOs can act as employer or principal and there is no need for appointees to undertake these roles. This distinction leads to a major difference in the responsibilities which appointees owe in relation to the acts of employees or agents under situation (b) above.

Corporate structures

A150 Appointees in corporate structures will not be responsible for any acts of the PSO's agents or employees which cause loss to the PSO (situation (a)), unless (i) the appointees have personally ordered or procured the act which has led to the loss (making them joint parties to the act), or (ii) a breach of the appointees' skill and care duties can be said to have caused the loss. In the first situation the appointee could be subject to any criminal liability which arises from the particular conduct; and in both situations the PSO would have rights against the appointees for failure to perform their responsibilities to the PSO, as outlined earlier in this chapter.

A151 In the case of acts of agents or employees which harm third parties (situation (b)), the PSO as principal or employer will have to share liability to the third party with the individual agent or

employee. This is because the laws governing agency and employment relationships specify that a principal and an employer can be liable for the acts of their agents or employees respectively (often called 'vicarious liability').[178] In both cases the agent or employee must be acting within the scope of their authority or employment before the PSO can be fixed with liability. Once this is established however, the third party can proceed against the individual or the PSO or both, to recover compensation for the harm they have suffered.[179]

A152 However, since the PSO itself is fixed with the vicarious liability, appointees in corporate PSOs are not potentially liable to third parties for such acts, unless they have participated in the wrongdoing by ordering or procuring the wrong or actually performing the act.[180]

Non-corporate structures

A153 For non-corporate structures when an employee or agent causes loss to the PSO itself (situation (a)), the position is similar to that for corporate appointees discussed above: if the act is a personal act of the appointee jointly with the agent or employee, personal liability will arise. Equally, if the appointee fails to exercise adequate skill and care then potential liability can arise. This latter proposition is well developed for trustees, who must ensure that they act in good faith when appointing an agent, and that they exercise appropriate care in oversight of the agent's work.[181]

A154 In situation (b), because the PSO is not the employer or principal, it is the individual appointees who bear any responsibilities imposed by law for the acts of employees or agents. Therefore, where the law states that employers or principals are vicariously liable for harm caused

---

[177] This distinction assumes the employee is not also authorised as an agent.

[178] See *Bowstead & Reynolds on Agency* (1996 16th ed) and *Harvey on Industrial Relations and Employment Law* (looseleaf work) for details of these rules.

[179] But see Chapter 6 on the protection available in theses circumstances, including a possible indemnity from the employee for the benefit of the employer: *Lister v Romford Ice and Cold Storage Co* [1957] AC 555.

[180] But see paragraphs B18 ff below and Appendix C for concerns that this separation between appointee and PSO may not always be complete.

[181] *Re Vickery* [1931] 1 Ch 572 and Trustee Act 1925 ss 23,30(1) – by virtue of which 'wilful default' must be proved on the part of trustees before they can be liable for the agent's conduct.

to third parties, it is the individual appointee who incurs this potential liability. Protection is specifically available for such appointees by means of insurance or indemnities (see Chapter 6).

Conclusions

A155 Responsibility for the wrongful acts of other people associated with the PSO is unlikely to result in personal liability for appointees unless they have become personally responsible for the particular conduct. However, in discharging the skill and care duty described in Duty Two above, appointees must give consideration to the degree of oversight which is required where other people are carrying out activities on behalf of appointees.

A156 Appointees in non-corporate structures need to be particularly aware of the potential for vicarious liability which exists as a result of the appointees' role as employer or principal.

Section B – Responsibilities owed to third parties

Introduction

B1 Section A above considered the responsibilities appointees owe to their PSO. It discussed an appointee's potential liability when their failure to fulfil a duty to the PSO adversely affects a transaction between the PSO and a third party, or causes harm to a third party. This section is concerned with the duties which are owed by appointees directly to third parties, under statute and at common law.

B2 All appointees will bear such responsibilities, not because of their service on a responsible body but simply as a result of their everyday activities. For example, all appointees will be aware of their duty not to injure other people or steal someone else's property. These are the duties of the ordinary citizen. This section (and indeed the study) is not concerned with this type of duty. Instead it looks at the duties (and potential liability) vis-à-vis third parties which result from appointees' service on a responsible body.[182]

B3 Whatever the size of a PSO, it will often be undertaking activities which bring it into contact with other organisations and members of the public. For example, a PSO may act as an employer, as an occupier of land, or as an organiser of public events. Whenever a PSO makes contact in this way, the law may step in and regulate the relationship between the PSO and the third party. The purpose of this regulation is not to target PSOs specifically; nor is it derived from the legal structure of the PSO. Rather, it is imposed uniformly throughout society, by statute and common law, for the benefit of individuals and the community at large. This 'social regulation' can produce both criminal and civil liabilities, and may lead to personal consequences for appointees, particularly in non-corporate structures.

---

[182] The question of duties owed to third party creditors in times of a PSO's insolvency are considered separately in Chapter 5 and Appendix D.

B4 The commentary which follows describes the types of social regulation which exist for the benefit of third parties who have dealings with PSOs. It then discusses when appointees in non-corporate and corporate structures respectively will be personally liable if a PSO's activities infringe such social regulation. Finally, the topics of judicial review and the criminal law generally are dealt with.

Social regulation

B5 Social regulation by statute is extensive and can impose duties between members of society in a wide variety of situations. For example, employment law imposes duties on employers to protect workers from discrimination and unfair dismissal;[183] health and safety law requires employers and occupiers of land to ensure safe premises for employees and visitors;[184] and licensing laws impose requirements which regulate the conduct of fundraising events involving lotteries or the consumption of alcohol.[185] Such statutory social regulation can create both civil and criminal offences.

B6 Since statutory regulation is designed to ensure good behaviour as well as provide redress for injured third parties, these duties can be owed to society generally as well as to individuals. Thus, while individual employees are given statutory rights to remedy an unfair dismissal, much health and safety legislation is enforced by the state.

Therefore, in many cases there does not need to be an actual injured third party to show breach of a duty; the potential for a third party to be harmed will suffice.[186]

B7 The common law also imposes social regulation in a wide variety of situations, based upon the general principle that people should be prevented "from hurting one another, whether in respect of their property, their persons, their reputations, or anything else which is theirs".[187] This gives rise to the law of tort.

B8 This principle leads to a range of different legal duties being imposed upon people and organisations: e.g. the duty not to cause damage and the duty to take care.[188] Failure to fulfil these duties (known as tortious acts) gives rise to potential civil liabilities to third parties in the form of financial compensation.[189] Examples include cases where third parties are personally injured by a PSO's activities, or suffer trespass or nuisance to their person or property, or are libelled or slandered.[190]

B9 The extent to which statutory or common law social regulation applies to a PSO will depend upon its size and the functions it is carrying out. Where any of the types of regulation described above do apply, the rules which determine whether an appointee will be personally liable for a failure to comply with them will vary depending on the legal structure of the PSO.

---

[183] See, for example, the Sex Discrimination Acts 1975 and 1986; the Disability Discrimination Act 1996; Employment Rights Act 1996.

[184] See, for example, the Health and Safety at Work etc Act 1974 and the various regulations made thereunder; the Occupiers' Liability Acts 1957 and 1984.

[185] See, for example, the Licensing Act 1964 and the Licensing (Occasional Permissions) Act 1983; the Lotteries and Amusements Act 1976; the National Lottery etc Act 1993.

[186] See the case of *R v Board of Trustees of the Science Museum* [1993] 3 All ER 853 where the Court of Appeal held that exposure to risk in the health and safety context (breach of s.3(1) of the 1974 Act) meant the possibility of danger arising and not actual danger.

[187] *Salmond & Heuston on the Law of Torts* (21st ed 1996) p13.

[188] Most but not all torts are based on the duty not to cause damage. Torts involving negligence require a duty of care also.

[189] Strictly speaking, 'damages'.

[190] These areas of law are not without statutory rules, but the foundation of the duty remains one of common law.

Non-corporate structures

B10 Due to a non-corporate PSO's lack of legal personality, it will be the appointees themselves in these structures who will be undertaking the activities which are the subject of statutory social regulation. For example, appointees rather than the PSO will be the employers of any staff, the responsible organisers of fundraising events, and the occupiers of premises and land.[191] This means that any social regulation associated with such functions will apply to appointees personally, and failure to fulfil the requisite duties will produce a potential personal liability.[192]

B11 In terms of the common law duties, again, as the PSO has no legal personality, any damage associated with a PSO's activities and caused to a third party will have to be attributed to an individual rather than the PSO itself. Whether this individual is an appointee will depend on the facts of the case. If the conduct giving rise to the damage is the appointee's own, then responsibility will lie with them.

B12 If the conduct is someone else's, then appointees may still be 'vicariously liable', as described under Section A, Duty Five above: trustees are not automatically responsible for loss caused to the trust by an agent, unless they themselves are at fault in their employment and oversight of that agent. Trustees are, on the other hand, vicariously liable for the wrongful acts of their employees or agents which harm third parties. Committee members of unincorporated associations are also vicariously liable for the acts of employees but, unlike trustees, are also liable for the acts of agents.

B13 If the person causing injury to the third party is neither acting as an appointee, an agent nor an employee then the conduct cannot be related to the activities of the PSO, and will become a matter to be dealt with between the parties as ordinary citizens.

Corporate structures

B14 In corporate structures the position is very different because the PSO has a legal personality to which the requirements of social regulation can attach. Thus it is the PSO which is employer, occupier of land, and organiser of events, and any failure to fulfil these responsibilities can generally be laid at the door of the PSO in the first instance. Equally, a PSO is quite capable at law of being liable for damage it causes to third parties in breach of its common law duties not to harm others.[193]

B15 However, that said, personal liability for failure to comply with social regulation can become an issue for appointees in corporate structures. Three situations need to be considered.

B16 First, some forms of statutory regulation stipulate that people in a corporate organisation who have a particular responsibility for a matter can be made personally liable for a failure to comply with relevant regulations. The main form of regulation relevant to PSOs in this context is health and safety law.[194] However, such personal liability will only be imposed where the responsible individual is in some way culpable of the failure (and appointees will escape liability, in the health and safety context, if they can show that they took all reasonably practical steps to prevent whatever

---

[191] In unincorporated associations there may be a separate group of trustees (as opposed to committee members) who are responsible for the property of the association.

[192] But see Chapter 6 below for the protection available to non-corporate appointees where they are acting for the PSO's purposes and within the scope of their authority.

[193] Such harm will have been caused by a natural person, e.g. an employee or an agent, but the liability can be that of the corporate PSO where (a) an action would lie against an individual; (b) the person committing the damage was acting within the scope of their authority; and (c) (probably) the act was not *ultra vires:* see Appendix C.

[194] See for example s.37 Health and Safety at Work etc Act 1974 rendering appointees who have connived in or consented to the commission of an offence by the PSO under the statute (or whose neglect contributed to the offence) personally liable. Other examples of such provisions include Food Safety Act 1990 s.36; Environmental Protection Act 1990 s.157.

situation has given rise to the prosecution).[195] The definition of culpability will vary depending on the terms of the statute.

B17 Second, if appointees themselves perform acts which contravene the common law duties described above (e.g. they libel someone), then it needs to be ascertained as a matter of fact whether the appointee was acting in a personal capacity or legitimately on behalf of the PSO. Acts which are wilful or motivated by malice will be personal ones. Equally, where an appointee orders or procures an employee of a PSO to commit a tortious act, then, as described under Section A Duty Five above, personal liability will arise here also.[196] The fact that the act has been committed in relation to the PSO's affairs does not provide an immediate answer to the question of liability. This is particularly true where the harm is caused by a tortious act. A careful assessment of the facts needs to be made. In cases of contract it will be much clearer that the PSO is responsible, since the corporate PSO will be the contracting party.[197] This is still a developing area of the law, but generally when acting personally, the consequences of an appointee's acts will rest with the appointee alone.[198]

B18 The third situation which needs to be discussed is more complex, because it involves conflicting interpretations of the law. Appendix C sets out a detailed legal analysis of the law on corporate acts. It shows that there is concern in some PSOs that appointees can be personally liable for the wrongful acts of the PSO jointly with the PSO.

B19 The generally held view of the law in this respect is that the PSO and an appointee cannot both be liable for the same event; the duty to be owed (and any corresponding liability) will be placed upon one or other of them, and moreover will only fall to appointees if they are acting personally (the second situation outlined above). Thus, there is a vital distinction between corporate acts and personal acts. However, this position is in contrast to the law which governs employees or agents of a corporate PSO where there can be joint duties owed by both parties and both or either may be rendered liable for any harm caused by breach of those duties.[199] This has led to concern that the generally held view may not, in fact, be legally secure.

B20 Appendix C sets out more fully the different legal propositions involved in this problem, and highlights the difficulties it raises.

Crimes

B21 While statutory social regulation can create criminal offences, most people understand the word 'crime' to mean acts such as theft, assault or murder. In a study of the personal liability of appointees very little needs to be said about this aspect of the criminal law.

B22 In most contexts crimes will be the personal acts of an individual, and if that individual is an appointee, then the appointee is subject to the criminal justice system, as any citizen would be. It is possible for a crime to be committed by a PSO with a corporate structure,[200] provided the offence is not one for which the sole penalty is death or imprisonment (e.g. murder), or which cannot be committed vicariously (e.g. by another person on its behalf). However, this does not mean an appointee will necessarily be jointly liable for a corporate crime.

---

[195] And see *R v Gateway Foodmarkets* [1997] 3 All ER 78 for a recent Court of Appeal judgment confirming the reasonable practicability defence as the only constraint on the otherwise strict liability (for an offence under section 2(1)).

[196] See *C Evans Ltd v Spritebrand Ltd* [1985] 1 WLR 317.

[197] See Duty A1 above on responsibility to act in place of the PSO.

[198] If an appointee is an agent or employee of the PSO, then notwithstanding that the act is a personal act, the PSO could be vicariously liable, but this does not diminish the ultimate personal liability of the appointee: see *Lloyd v Grace Smith & Co* [1912] AC 716; *Racz v Home Office* [1994] 2 AC 45.

[199] Although ultimately the employee owes an indemnity to the employer: see footnote 179 above.

[200] Without a legal personality non-corporate structures cannot be guilty of a criminal offence, except in exceptional circumstances, where a statute specifies that an offence can be committed by a non-corporate body.

B23 Much has been written about the offence of 'corporate manslaughter' and other crimes which require a particular state of mind to be exhibited in order to prove guilt. The question was whether an organisation could have a state of mind. As the law has developed it has become clear that the 'controlling minds' of a corporate structure (in most cases the responsible body) are capable of supplying the necessary state of mind (*mens rea*) for a criminal offence.[201] This means that a corporate structure can, in theory, commit crimes which demand intention or neglect (they have always been potentially liable for strict liability offences).

B24 For appointees also to be personally liable for such a crime the criminal conduct must have been the personal act of the appointee. At the point where criminal proceedings are brought against a corporate structure however, responsible individuals are also likely to be subject to prosecution.

Judicial review

B25 Many of the PSOs studied are subject to supervisory jurisdiction by the higher courts over their decision-making processes. Under this jurisdiction (which is exercisable by application for judicial review), the court applies principles of administrative law to the decisions or acts of the PSO, and has power to set aside decisions or restrain acts which are illegal or irrational or which are procedurally unfair. The courts may also give declaratory judgments as to the rights of the parties or, exceptionally, award financial redress to injured parties.

B26 The courts are able to entertain an application for judicial review where the PSO is undertaking public law functions rather than private law activities, e.g. exercising statutory powers or performing public duties. In practice, all PSOs which are statutory corporations are subject to this jurisdiction (unless statute expressly excludes it), and NDPBs with different legal structures will also be covered.[202]

B27 However, applications for judicial review are not essentially concerned with the personal liability of the people taking the particular decision or act, but with denying the effect of the unlawful conduct. Thus, the forms of relief available are not addressed to imposing penalties upon individuals, but seek to remedy any misuse of power or other unlawful conduct.

B28 Judicial review applications have increased rapidly over recent years.[203] However, it is not apparent that the procedure is being used to impose personal liability on members of decision-making bodies. Even if a PSO is found to have made an invalid decision, it does not follow that the PSO, still less its appointees, would be liable in damages. For such damages to be awarded, it would need to be shown that the PSO acted in bad faith in exercising its powers or that its behaviour constituted a tort or a breach of contract. For personal liability of the appointee to arise, the unlawful act would have to have been done in such bad faith, that it could not be said to be have been done on behalf of the PSO.

Misuse of public office

B29 Where appointees hold public office or exercise public functions they are subject to legal provisions regulating misuse of their powers, namely the criminal offence of misconduct in public office and the tort of misfeasance in public office. Appointees in NDPBs will be subject to these provisions, as may appointees in statutory or chartered corporations, depending on the nature of their powers.

---

[201] See *Tesco Supermarkets Ltd v Nattrass* [1972] AC 153.

[202] For further details of the law and procedure see Wade and Forsyth *Administrative Law* (7th ed 1994); Supperstone and Goudie *Judicial Review* (1991).

[203] See the statistics contained in the Law Commission Consultation Paper No 126 *Administrative Law: Judicial Review and Statutory Appeals* (1993) at paragraph 2.14.

B30 The criminal offence, which is common law not statutory, does not require dishonesty on the part of the appointee, but there must be some improper, oppressive or dishonest motive in the exercise or refusal to exercise a public function.[204] The tort of misfeasance, by virtue of which parties injured can recover compensation, is concerned with the deliberate and dishonest wrongful abuse of power.[205] Prosecutions and civil actions are rare, and provided appointees exercise their public functions in good faith, i.e. honestly and reasonably, neither aspect of misuse of public office will result in personal liability for appointees.

B31 The Committee on Standards in Public Life recommended that a new statutory offence of misuse of public office should be introduced, developed from the existing common law offence.[206] A Consultation Paper was issued, and the Law Commission and the Home Office are taking forward work on this issue presently.[207] One of the matters being addressed is the extent to which any new offence should include office-holders of organisations not presently included within the scope of the common law offence, e.g. further and higher education institutions or grant-maintained schools. At present there is no indication of whether a new offence will be developed as recommended.

Conclusions

B32 Social regulation encompasses a wide and diverse body of law, and the above section has given an overview of the different types of regulation which exist. However, it can be seen that failure to comply with the required standards of conduct (whether imposed by statute or common law) can result in potential personal liability for appointees in corporate and non-corporate structures. For the most part the law is clear and guidance is available for appointees on their responsibilities.

B33 Appointees in non-corporate structures are likely to be undertaking many more activities which make them directly responsible to third parties than their counterparts in corporate structures. It is important that such appointees understand the nature of the role they are fulfilling personally. Specific protection is available for these appointees (indemnities and/or insurance), although it can have its limitations.[208]

B34 In corporate structures, the starting point for appointees is that they can be made liable under social regulation if they are personally responsible for the particular wrongful act or omission in question. However, the uncertainty over an appointee's joint liability for corporate acts (highlighted in Appendix C) makes it impossible to give definitive guidance about where to draw the line between personal acts and corporate acts. In an increasingly litigious society, this makes it more difficult to reassure appointees in corporate structures that social regulation will only attach to their own personal acts.

---

[204] *R v Dytham* [1979] QB 722.

[205] *Three Rivers DC v Bank of England (No 3)* [1996] 3 All ER 558.

[206] *Standards of Conduct in Local Government* (Cm 3702-I July 1997) Recommendation 28. The recommendation, while relating to all holders of public office, was linked to the abolition of surcharge.

[207] *Misuse of Public Office: A New Offence?* July 1997.

[208] As described in Chapter 6.

Section C – Responsibilities owed to regulators

Introduction

C1 In addition to the duties owed by PSOs to third parties in general, they have responsibilities to their regulators. These responsibilities are designed to ensure proper administration and financial accountability and will, in the first instance, be placed upon the responsible body collectively. Such regulation may arise from the legal structure of the PSO, or it may result from the particular type of public benefit which the PSO provides. Because of this, some PSOs have more than one regulator.

C2 It is important that appointees understand the requirements placed upon their responsible body by regulators, since they can be held personally liable for failure to comply with regulatory requirements. Regulators also have a role to play in relation to an appointee's disqualification from office, and this is discussed below.

Identity of regulators

C3 Table 1 gives details of the main regulators which oversee the work of the different types of PSO studied. It does not give details of regulators who have responsibilities for standards, e.g. OFSTED, since their powers do not raise issues of personal liability for appointees.

Role of regulators

C4 The roles of the regulators identified in Table 1 vary greatly. Four different types of regulation can be distinguished.

C5 The first type involves carrying out registration and ensuring that statutory formalities such as filing of accounts are complied with. However, it does not involve active investigation or regulation of the internal management of PSOs. The Registrar of Companies is an example of this type of regulator.

C6 The second type involves a more active role in overseeing the activities of the PSO, as well as registration functions. Such regulators have powers to institute investigations when financial or managerial problems arise. However, they do not provide any funds for the PSO. The Charity Commission and the Registrar of Friendly Societies are examples of this type of body.[209]

C7 The third type involves regulation by bodies which provide funds to PSOs for a particular public benefit. Here the funding bodies lay down detailed requirements about how the funds are to be used (together with accounting and auditing requirements). For example, government departments providing funds to NDPBs set out such requirements in a Financial Memorandum, and the Funding Agency for Schools and the Funding Councils for Higher and Further Education similarly attach conditions to their grants,[210] thereby exercising regulatory control.[211] However, these regulators do not carry out any registration functions, since the PSOs they regulate do not require it.

C8 The Housing Corporation is a hybrid of the second and third types of regulation, as it provides funds for registered social landlords, and also carries out registration functions and has investigatory responsibilities.

---

[209] Of the two, the Charity Commission has the more proactive role in the regulation of PSOs.

[210] It is accepted that the funding role of these bodies is the primary purpose for which they are established, and they are not necessarily perceived as true regulators. However, their role in relation to the use of the PSO's funds and the provision of information makes these bodies more than passive funders. Standing behind this type of regulator will be the Secretary of State from the relevant government department (e.g. Health or Education and Employment), who will also have certain rights in relation to the administration of the PSO.

[211] The regulators of local authority maintained schools will be the local authority itself through the LMS scheme, and the district auditor, so far as the school is spending a delegated budget.

Table 1

Public service organisation	Regulator: associated with a legal structure	Regulator: associated with a particular public benefit[212]
Grant maintained schools		Funding Agency for Schools
Registered social landlords	The Registrar of Friendly Societies	The Housing Corporation
Further education colleges		Further Education Funding Councils for England and for Wales
TECs	Registrar of Companies	Secretary of State for Education and Employment[213]
Post-1992 universities		Higher Education Funding Councils for England and for Wales
Pre-1992 universities	Visitatorial jurisdiction[214]	Higher Education Funding Councils for England and for Wales
Local authority maintained schools	The District Auditor	The local authority
Registered charities	If a charitable company: Registrar of Companies	The Charity Commission
NHS trusts		Secretary of State for Health and NHS Executive
Executive NDPBs	If a company: Registrar of Companies	Parent government department

C9 Fourth, there is the type of regulation exercised by the Visitor of chartered corporations, which is unique in terms of regulation of PSOs. The Visitor is the judge of the internal laws of an eleemosynary corporation (i.e. most pre-1992 universities) and has almost exclusive jurisdiction to determine disputes or problems relating to these laws. Thus where questions arise about the management of the corporation's property or construction of the terms of the governing instruments, it is the Visitor who usually rules definitively on such matters.[215]

---

[212] Not including audit regulators – see paragraph C11 below.

[213] This regulation is derived from the contract which the DfEE places with TECs in order for them to perform public services. See Appendix A for details.

[214] See paragraph C9 ff below.

[215] The exception being (a) where statute has overridden the Visitor's exclusive jurisdiction, e.g. s.206 Education Reform Act 1988 which removes the jurisdiction of the Visitor to hear many employment matters; and (b) where the matter concerns the general common law, rather than the specific domestic laws of the corporation. This means that matters pertaining to property held on trust by the corporation fall to the courts, not the Visitor, to determine.

C10 The office of Visitor will usually be carried out by a judge appointed by the Lord Chancellor where the Crown is the official Visitor. The Visitor has power to award compensation,[216] and there is no appeal from the Visitor to the courts, except in very limited circumstances by way of judicial review.[217] Unlike all other types of regulation discussed above, where if problems arise between PSO and regulator or appointee and regulator it will be for the courts to decide the matter ultimately, for chartered corporations it may be the Visitor who is allotted this task.

C11 Finally, in addition to these four types of regulator, many PSOs are subject to audit supervision: NDPBs, NHS trusts, statutory corporations and TECs all fall within the remit of either the National Audit Office or the Audit Commission to a greater or lesser extent.[218] Parliamentary Select Committees also have powers to scrutinise the work of these PSOs.

Regulatory requirements

C12 Each regulator will have their own specific requirements with which the responsible body of the PSO must ensure compliance. Some requirements will derive direct from statute, others will come from rules developed by regulators using powers given to them for the purpose. The range of such responsibilities is too great to be summarised in this study; information on the details of these requirements is available from the regulators themselves. However, the text which follows highlights some of the common administration requirements of the regulatory regimes for PSOs.

C13 Where a PSO is required to register with a regulator, detailed rules about how this is achieved and keeping the register up to date will be set down. Keeping records of members' details by the PSO itself may also be a requirement, as with industrial and provident societies.[219] These are the types of requirement which can impose particular administrative costs and burdens upon PSOs, and which are regarded as unsuitable for many smaller organisations, prompting the pressure for reform discussed at paragraphs A13–16 above.

C14 Most PSOs are required to prepare and publish or supply to a regulator financial accounts,[220] which in many instances will also need to be externally audited.[221] Detailed rules about the form of such accounts and their presentation will be stipulated by regulators, or a best practice recommended. There may also be requirements to publish annual reports or returns about the activities of the PSO. Some PSOs are under a statutory obligation to lay their accounts before Parliament.[222] What regulators do with this information varies. Some, such as the Registrar of Companies, will undertake no analysis of the accounts but simply act as a repository for public record. Others will use the information to scrutinise the performance of the PSO, e.g. the funding authorities of statutory corporations.

C15 The duty to furnish accounts and annual returns is an important one and failure to comply with these requirements can have personal consequences for appointees in some legal structures, as described below.

---

[216] *Thomas v University of Bradford* [1987] AC 795, 823F–824B.

[217] *R v Lord President of the Council ex p. Page* [1993] AC 682.

[218] This supervision may be in the form of a full financial audit, e.g. for most NDPBs, or it may be limited to a value-for-money audit (necessitating inspection rights), e.g. for further and higher education institutions.

[219] Industrial and Provident Societies Act 1965 s.44.

[220] Local authority maintained schools have a less onerous requirement in this respect than the other types of PSO studied, because they come under the 'umbrella' of the authority, by means of a delegated budget. However, they must supply the local authority with regular and accurate records of expenditure and income.

[221] For some PSOs there is a threshold of income, below which unaudited accounts will suffice, e.g. registered charities whose income or expenditure is under £10,000 p.a.

[222] Most NDPBs must do this, and NHS trusts individually must deposit reports and accounts with the Parliamentary libraries.

C16 Some regulators have a role in ensuring that the purposes for which the PSO's funds are applied are proper under the terms of the PSO's governing instruments. Regulators of types 2 and 3 above will be concerned with this, and their investigatory powers brought into action if necessary. Equally the manner in which finances are obtained can be subject to regulation. The liability which may arise for appointees from these responsibilities has been discussed in the sections on governance and fiduciary responsibilities in Section A above.

C17 It is important that PSOs which are subject to more than one regulatory jurisdiction understand how the requirements overlap. Table 1 shows where more than one body has responsibility for aspects of a PSO's affairs. For example, charitable companies are subject to the jurisdiction of the Charity Commission and the Registrar of Companies. Usually rules are put in place to avoid cumbersome double regulation, e.g. charitable companies are exempted from most of the Charity Commission's requirements on accounts, and exempt charities have minimal duties in this respect.[223]

Potential liability

C18 The administrative requirements described above will be placed upon the responsible body in the first instance. They are well-publicised requirements, and it will be difficult for responsible bodies to fail to comply properly with them (although professional advice may be necessary). However, in some legal structures appointees can be made personally liable for such failure, as the following discussion explains.

C19 Appointees to companies, industrial and provident societies, and trusts or unincorporated associations registered as charities with the Charity Commission are at risk of personal liability in certain circumstances. For all three types of body specific offences can be committed by appointees personally if the PSO fails to comply with the accounting and reporting requirements of the Charity Commission, the Registrar of Companies or the Registrar of Friendly Societies, as appropriate.[224] To be liable it will be necessary to show that the appointee knowingly or wilfully authorised or permitted the failure, and it will be a question of fact whether a particular appointee has been given responsibility for compliance, or whether all appointees collectively are responsible. Committing the offence renders appointees liable to a fine, or, in exceptional circumstances for appointees to companies, imprisonment.[225]

C20 However, such offences will only be committed where there is no reasonable excuse for the appointee's failure, and in the case of registered charities the failure must also be persistent. Therefore, a single failure due to a genuine and honest mistake is highly unlikely to give rise to a personal liability.

C21 For statutory and chartered corporations the situation is somewhat different. If a responsible body in one of these PSOs fails to discharge its administrative responsibilities to its regulators there are no specific offences leading to the imposition of fines upon appointees.[226] Personal liability does not result from appointees' failure to file proper accounts etc, unless a breach of a fiduciary or governance duty is also involved.[227]

---

[223] The Charities Act 1993 expressly relieves charitable companies and exempt charities from many of the accounting provisions that otherwise apply to registered charities.

[224] Companies Act 1985 ss.221(5), 730(5); Charities Act 1993 s.49; Industrial and Provident Societies Act 1965 s.61; Friendly and Industrial and Provident Societies Act 1968 ss.18,21.

[225] An offence concerning failure to take reasonable steps to ensure the accuracy of accounts is also created for committee members of industrial and provident societies (with a financial penalty): s.3(7) Friendly and Industrial and Provident Societies Act 1968.

[226] This is because these types of requirements are not set out in statute, as they are for registered charities, companies and industrial and provident societies (enabling offences to be created), but instead are developed as conditions of the grants which the regulators are providing to the PSOs.

[227] Governing instruments make differing requirements as to the administrative procedures with which responsible bodies must comply.

However, since the regulators of these PSOs are also their funders, failure to comply with administrative requirements can lead to investigations of the PSO's affairs, and requirements that the failure be remedied.

Disqualification from office

C22 While the preceding discussion has focused on particular responsibilities owed by responsible bodies to regulators, mention also needs to be made of the general powers of regulators in relation to the removal or disqualification from office of appointees.[228]

C23 As described in Chapter 2, this study assumes that appointees have been properly appointed and that they fulfil any qualification criteria specified for the appointment.[229] Accordingly, appointees will expect to relinquish office through voluntary resignation,[230] death, or completion of tenure.[231] Nonetheless, removal from office and disqualification from further service are potential consequences for appointees who fail to fulfil properly the responsibilities described in this chapter.[232] Removal from office will occur if there has been a wrongful act by an appointee or if they are judged to be unfit for office; and disqualification will be ordered only in exceptional circumstances for culpable conduct by an appointee.

C24 However, it should not be assumed that either consequence will arise automatically when a potential personal liability arises for an appointee. For example, as described earlier, trustees incur personal liability quite legitimately when acting in place of a trust PSO, and there is no question of removal from office here. It will depend in all cases on the circumstances and the extent to which there has been wrongdoing by an appointee.

C25 The text below provides an overview of the powers of PSOs and regulators in relation to removal and disqualification. It is not a complete summary of the law, but gives an outline of the types of powers which exist.

C26 PSOs themselves can have powers in their governing instruments to remove appointees from office, although this will never extend to a power to disqualify the appointee from serving generally in that capacity. That jurisdiction will be exercised by a regulator or the courts.

C27 Where a PSO does have such powers they will be tightly drawn to ensure that appointees cannot be removed for trivial or ill-motivated reasons. For example, the governing instruments of grant maintained schools and local authority maintained schools permit removal where there has been chronic non-attendance by an appointee, or where they become bankrupt, or are convicted of a criminal offence;[233] governors in further education colleges can be removed for these reasons, and where it is judged that they are unable or unfit to discharge their functions.[234] In both these examples it is the responsible body which exercises these powers.

C28 Where, in corporate structures or unincorporated associations, the membership is wider than the responsible body, the governing instruments may provide rules for the circumstances in which members collectively may remove appointees from office.

---

[228] Removal can be used to cover cases where the appointee wishes to be removed, but is not used in this context here.

[229] E.g. there are often age-ranges within which an appointee must fall and restrictions on the appointment of persons who are bankrupt or have criminal convictions.

[230] The governing instruments of each PSO will describe how resignation is to be handled. In some cases (e.g. trusts) it is usual for a replacement trustee to be appointed at the same time; whereas in the other legal structures the vacancy can be filled at a later date.

[231] Many PSOs prevent appointees from serving longer than a given period of years.

[232] And assuming no relief is granted to the appointee, as described in Chapter 6 below.

[233] For the details of which see respectively The Education (Grant-maintained Schools) (Initial Governing Instruments) Regulations 1993, as amended, and The Education (School Government) Regulations 1989 as amended.

[234] Education (Government of Further Education Corporations) Regulations 1992 Sch 1 Instruments 7, 9 (SI 1992/1963 as amended).

C29 The powers which regulators have in this respect (as opposed to PSOs) vary. They can have the power to remove and/or to disqualify.

C30 Some regulators have powers to intervene in the affairs of the PSO and replace the appointees in the event of mismanagement or breach of duty. The Charity Commission has such powers for appointees to registered charities;[235] the Housing Corporation for registered social landlords;[236] and the Secretary of State for Education and Employment retains such powers in the case of further education colleges.[237] Where the Charity Commission exercises its power of removal, the appointee is automatically disqualified from further service on a responsible body of a charity.[238]

C31 For other regulators the sanction of the court is needed before disqualification will take effect for individual appointees. In the case of companies, disqualification proceedings and a court order are necessary to disqualify a director from future office.[239] Equally the courts have an inherent jurisdiction in the case of registered and exempt charities to order the removal of a trustee, and in this case again the appointee will automatically be disqualified from future appointment.[240]

C32 It can be seen therefore that removal and disqualification are not types of personal liability which will befall an appointee for *any* failure to fulfil the responsibilities described in this study. Rather, they will become an issue when the appointees are judged to be truly failing in their responsibilities, for whatever reason.

Conclusions

C33 The above is no more than an overview of regulatory powers, but there are general conclusions to be reached in relation to appointees' potential liability. The functions of regulators vary between the different types of PSO, depending on the legal structure, and the public benefit provided, but each requires appointees to comply with administrative rules concerning the conduct of the PSO. Personal liability for failure to comply with these rules will only arise where appointees are guilty of culpable failure in discharging their duties.

C34 There is considerable guidance for appointees on the requirements of regulators and professional help is available to ensure responsible bodies can comply with their duties. In general this is not an area where appointees should fear personal liability being imposed without good reason.

C35 The possibility of removal from office or disqualification from further service is a remote risk. Where it does arise it will be for culpable misconduct by the appointee, and not for insubstantial reasons. Indeed, imposition of a personal liability without an act of bad faith on the part of the appointee (e.g. where a non-corporate appointee is acting in place of the PSO: Duty One in Section A above) should not involve any question of removal from office.

---

[235] Charities Act 1993 ss 16,18.

[236] Housing Act 1996 Schedule 1 Part II.

[237] Further and Higher Education Act 1992 s.57.

[238] Charities Act 1993 s.72.

[239] See Company Directors Disqualification Act 1986 on the procedures and the reasons permitting disqualification.

[240] *Letterstedt v Broers* (1844) 9 App Cas 371; Charities Act 1993 s.72(d)(iii).

Chapter 5 – Insolvency: duties and responsibilities

Introduction

5.1 The duties described in Chapter 4 are those that apply to appointees during their stewardship of a PSO provided it is solvent. When a PSO is threatened with a situation where its debts exceed its assets (or simply runs out of money), the law can impose further burdens on appointees, beyond those described above.

5.2 Appointees will have two concerns if their PSO runs out of money:

    (a) their liability for the fact that the PSO has become insolvent under their stewardship; and

    (b) their liability to third parties owed money by the insolvent PSO.[241]

5.3 To answer the first concern, appointees need to consider the reason for the insolvency, and the duties they owed generally while part of the responsible body. To answer the second, appointees need to look at the legal structure of their PSO. Before turning to both these matters, the general effect of insolvency upon a PSO needs to be considered briefly.

The effect of insolvency

5.4 Running out of money does not mean that a PSO will automatically cease to exist. As described in Chapter 3, positive steps usually need to be taken to dissolve a PSO whatever its legal structure.[242] Moreover, dissolution can take place where a PSO has been a success (e.g. because the purpose it has been set up to achieve has been fulfilled), as well as a failure.

5.5 However, insolvency will make it impossible for the PSO to carry on any practical tasks. Usually steps will be taken to dissolve it, initiated either by the appointees or members themselves or, in some cases, by third parties owed money by the PSO. The law provides a number of different methods for dealing with this situation, depending on the legal structure of the PSO.

5.6 Insolvent companies and industrial and provident societies can be wound up voluntarily or compulsorily by order of the court.[243] In both cases detailed statutory provisions deal with the procedure for winding up, the appointment of a liquidator and the satisfaction of the PSO's debts.[244] Further, where a PSO is a charitable company a winding-up petition may be presented by the Charity Commissioners or the Attorney General.[245]

5.7 Chartered corporations can be dissolved by a number of means, although in practice they are rarely used. A charter can be surrendered voluntarily by the corporation, forfeited or revoked. Revocation will usually be achieved by Act of Parliament, and the consent of the corporation itself is probably necessary for this. Forfeiture will apply where there has been misuse of the corporation's powers.[246] In theory any of

---

[241] While 'insolvency' has a technical meaning at law, it is used in this chapter as a generic term to describe the situation in any PSO (including non-corporate PSOs) where its liabilities exceed its assets.

[242] The exception is the unincorporated association which can be subject to 'spontaneous dissolution' – see Warburton *Unincorporated Associations* (2nd ed 1992) p102.

[243] There are two types of voluntary winding up, both initiated by the company itself, but giving differing rights to creditors where the company is insolvent: see Insolvency Act 1986 Part IV and Totty and Jordan *Insolvency* (looseleaf work) Part E for a detailed discussion of the different types of liquidation process.

[244] Insolvency Act 1986 Part IV and Insolvency Rules SI 1986/1925. The procedure for administrative receivership is not considered in the study.

[245] See s.63 of the Charities Act 1993. Where, upon dissolution and satisfaction of creditors, surplus property remains, the governing instruments of a charitable company usually specify that it is to be transferred to another charity, and not to the members, overriding s.154 Insolvency Act 1986: *Liverpool & District Hospital for Diseases of the Heart v AG* [1981] 1 Ch 193.

[246] For discussion of the various methods of dissolution see *Halsbury's Laws of England* (4th ed) vol 9 para 1390 ff.

these means could be used if a corporation became insolvent, although forfeiture is probably the least appropriate.[247]

5.8 For statutory corporations the founding legislation will deal with the method by which the corporation can be dissolved. Usually the relevant Secretary of State will have the right to dissolve the corporation by order, and to apportion the corporation's rights and liabilities to other similar organisations.[248] Often the statutory corporation may apply for dissolution, but the final decision is that of the Secretary of State.

5.9 Unincorporated associations may be wound up voluntarily by members' resolution (by a majority vote if the governing instruments provide power to do so; or unanimously if not), or by order of the court under its general equitable jurisdiction.[249] Where the association is a registered charity, the Charity Commissioner's permission will be needed to make an application to the court for the association to be wound up.[250]

5.10 Where a trust has insufficient funds to carry out its purpose, application can be made to the courts to alter the terms of the trust, to transfer its assets to another PSO, or to take other steps to ensure the effective use of the funds which are the subject of the trust, under the *cy-près* doctrine.[251] It is this ability to alter the purpose or terms of a trust that gives rise to the general proposition that a trust

for charitable purposes is perpetual. However, trusts can and will be terminated if insolvent, their affairs being wound up by the trustees, because a trust cannot exist without funds.[252] This will be the case even where the governing instruments contain no express power of termination (which will usually be the case). As indicated in Chapter 3 however, the fact that PSOs with a trust structure have permanent endowments makes it difficult for trustees to expend all the funds of the trust.[253]

(a) Duty to the PSO itself

5.11 In principle an appointee does not owe a duty to a PSO to prevent it becoming insolvent separate from the fiduciary and governance duties described in Chapter 4 for corporate and non-corporate structures. Therefore, if the cause of the insolvency is an appointee's failure to fulfil properly one of these duties, then the potential liability which may arise for that failure may include a claim for the consequences of the insolvency.[254]

5.12 The most obvious example of this will be where misappropriation of assets by an appointee leads to a PSO running out of money. In these circumstances, the PSO will have a claim against the appointee for breach of the fiduciary duties and for recovery of the assets, as described at paragraph A80 above. Depending on the facts of the case, there may also be the prospect of

---

[247] See *Halsbury's Laws op cit* para 1386 for a discussion of the use of *scire facias* proceedings for forfeiture of a charter.

[248] See, for example, s.27 Further and Higher Education Act 1992 and s.128 Education Reform Act 1988 (as amended) on dissolution of further and higher education corporations (post-1992 universities) respectively; and Sch 2, para 29 National Health Service and Community Care Act 1990 on dissolution of NHS trusts.

[249] *Re Lead Company's Workmen's Fund Society* [1904] 2 Ch 196. It has been assumed that the association, as a PSO, will not be subject to winding up under the Insolvency Act 1986 ss. 220–229 as an unregistered company, following *Re Bristol Athenaeum* (1889) 43 Ch D 236. However, to the extent that the PSO could be classed as a trading association then the winding up provisions would apply. See also paragraph 5.36 below and Appendix D.

[250] S.33 Charities Act 1993.

[251] See the discussion in *Tudor on Charities* (8th ed 1995) p453. The *cy-près* doctrine applies to other PSOs with charitable purposes, for example a chartered corporation which is a registered charity may apply for a *cy-près* scheme if there are insufficient funds or the purposes have altered: *Re Whitworth Art Gallery Trusts* [1958] 1 All ER 176.

[252] There is no equivalent to a liquidator for winding up a trust, but the Charity Commission has power to conduct an inquiry into the affairs of a registered charity if it is concerned about how the insolvency has arisen (s.8 Charities Act 1993); and may appoint additional trustees to wind up the trust (s.18 *ibid*). In exceptional circumstances the Official Solicitor can be appointed to wind up the trust.

[253] I.e. the trust has capital which is protected, and only income may be spent on the purposes of the PSO.

[254] Even the trustee, who is under the highest duty to preserve the assets of the trust (see paragraph A76 above), will not necessarily be personally liable for insolvency *per se,* unless a breach of another duty is also involved.

criminal proceedings if wrongdoing is involved. Equally, embarking on a reckless programme of expenditure, in opposition to professional advice, could breach the standards required from an appointee's skill and care duty.

5.13 While there may be no express duty placed upon appointees to ensure a PSO remains in funds *per se*, some governing instruments mention the need for the PSO to remain solvent. Thus, in the governing instruments of some statutory corporations there is a provision stating that the responsible body must look after the solvency of the institution it serves: see, for example, further education colleges.[255] NHS trusts also have a duty placed upon them to carry out their functions "effectively, efficiently and economically".[256]

5.14 Such duties are placed upon the responsible body as a whole, and not on the individual appointees. However, the expression of these duties has given cause for concern that where there has been no breach of the duties described in Chapter 4, the mere fact of insolvency could nonetheless render appointees liable for the consequences of insolvency.

5.15 While there has been no case testing the point, it seems unlikely that these terms in the governing instruments fix appointees with any additional duty, over and above those already owed. The governing instruments set down the guiding principles by which the responsible body is to conduct the stewardship of the PSO, and while appointees must, of course, pay heed to those principles when making decisions about the PSO, there is nothing in any of the provisions studied

in statutory corporations to suggest that the intent is to place an additional burden upon appointees.

5.16 Therefore, the presence of such a term in a PSO's governing instruments probably does not create an additional duty for appointees.

Is there anyone to enforce the duty?

5.17 Where a PSO does become insolvent, the question arises as to who may take action against an appointee if they believe the insolvency has been caused by an appointee's breach of fiduciary or governance duties.

5.18 The position in relation to losses caused to third parties upon insolvency is considered below. In terms of representing the PSO and bringing an action on its behalf, as already stated, the fact that a PSO becomes insolvent does not mean that it automatically ceases to exist at law. Usually any claims relating to the appointee's conduct will be dealt with during the winding-up process for both corporate and non-corporate PSOs.[257]

5.19 Therefore, even if insolvent, a PSO prior to dissolution can in theory proceed to enforce rights against an appointee (through fellow appointees or members).[258] However, a source of funds will be needed to finance a case, and this may be difficult to obtain.[259]

5.20 In the case of registered charities, the Charity Commission and the Attorney General can pursue an action against an appointee where the charity is insolvent, and a breach of duty is alleged.[260]

---

[255] The responsible body "shall be responsible for the effective and efficient use of resources, *the solvency of the institution and the Corporation and for safeguarding their assets*" – The Education (Government of Further Education Corporations) (Former Further Education Colleges) Regulations 1992 (1992/1963) (as amended) Sch 2 Art 3 (b) – (emphasis added).

[256] Paragraph 6, Schedule 2, Part II, National Health Service and Community Care Act 1990.

[257] For companies, the procedure supplied by s.212 Insolvency Act 1986 can be used to recover any property wrongfully received by the director, or to obtain any damages which the director owes the company for breach of the governance or fiduciary responsibilities.

[258] Obviously corporate structures can sue in the name of the PSO's legal personality, whereas non-corporate structures will need to have representative action taken by members, or appointees, on the basis of the trust or the member's contract as appropriate.

[259] Although in the event of a successful court action, the costs would be recoverable from the defendant appointee, to the extent that the appointee has the resources.

[260] See paragraphs 6.60 ff below for details of such 'charity proceedings'.

5.21 Once the PSO has been dissolved it is more difficult to identify who could pursue an appointee's breach of duty. If rights and liabilities have been transferred to another PSO (as will often be the case with statutory corporations for example), then it may be possible for that PSO to try and enforce any rights. However, it is for this reason that such claims are normally settled (by the courts) during the winding-up process.

(b) Duty to third parties

5.22 While there is no new duty owed to the PSO itself if it becomes insolvent, new potential liabilities do arise for some appointees in relation to third parties who are owed money by an insolvent PSO. Such duties are imposed for the protection of the PSO's creditors, rather than the punishment of the appointee, but their effect is to increase the burden upon appointees in some corporate PSOs.

Non-corporate structures

5.23 These additional duties are not imposed upon appointees to PSOs with non-corporate structures (trusts and unincorporated associations), since the lack of legal personality discussed earlier means that the PSO itself cannot owe money to anyone (it can have no creditors); instead, it will be the individual appointees acting in place of the PSO who will have entered into contracts, or undertaken tasks creating a financial obligation to a third party. So, as described earlier, it will always be their responsibility personally to discharge any liabilities to that third party whether the PSO is solvent or insolvent.[261]

5.24 However, the insolvency of a non-corporate PSO is not without consequences for an appointee, because the indemnification which they would usually enjoy to protect them from claims arising from personal acts in place of the PSO will become worthless if the PSO has no assets. This is described further in Chapter 6.[262]

5.25 A Consultation Paper issued by the Trust Law Committee *Rights of Creditors Against Trustees and Trust Funds*[263] provides a comparison of the law relating to creditors of trusts and creditors of companies. While considering trusts generally, and not only those which are registered charities, the paper raises options for reform, one of which is to strengthen the rights of creditors to have recourse direct against the trust fund. If such proposals were to be adopted it could reduce the need for actions against trustees personally, although not in all circumstances.[264]

Corporate structures

5.26 For appointees to corporate PSOs the situation is very different.

5.27 As explained in Chapter 3, the principle underlying the creation of a separate legal personality for a PSO is that the appointees to the responsible body enjoy limited liability: it is the PSO which is liable for debts and the appointees are not so liable beyond the sum which the appointee has 'guaranteed'.[265]

5.28 However, the protection afforded by limited liability is not all-embracing if a PSO has the structure of a company or an industrial and provident society, following reforms to the law in the 1980s to protect creditors of companies.

5.29 Furthermore, while statutory corporations and chartered corporations are not subject to the same rules which protect creditors, concerns have been

---

[261] Unless the appointees have made use of the protection discussed at paragraphs 6.47 ff below, namely exclusion clauses.

[262] At pp 79 ff below.

[263] April 1997.

[264] See the discussion in Chapter 4 *ibid*.

[265] The method of guarantee differs – in companies and industrial and provident societies a sum will be specified when the PSO is established (and see s.57 Industrial and Provident Societies Act 1965 and s.74 Insolvency Act 1986 on the liability of members in winding up); for chartered and statutory corporations, the presumption is that there is no liability to contribute to debts, unless the governing instruments state otherwise.

expressed about the position of statutory and chartered corporations by analogy with companies.

Wrongful trading

5.30 The Insolvency Act 1986 introduced a new legal remedy of 'wrongful trading', available to creditors of companies and industrial and provident societies.[266] Previously there had been means for creditors to secure recompense from directors of an insolvent company where there had been fraud on the directors' part. However, the new remedy was introduced to give creditors compensation where insolvency arose from a director's incompetence, rather than their deliberate fraud.[267]

5.31 The new remedy will arise (and impose liability upon a company director) where a company is in insolvent liquidation (i.e. being wound up), and the director, prior to the company's winding up, knew or ought to have concluded that there was no reasonable prospect that the company could avoid insolvent liquidation, but failed to take "every step" to minimise the potential loss to the company's creditors.[268] The action is brought by the liquidator of the company or society, on behalf of the individual creditors.

5.32 No dishonesty need be involved, since dishonest conduct in this regard is already covered by the offence of fraudulent trading. Instead, a court will compare the director's conduct to that of the reasonably diligent person having both the knowledge, skill and experience that might reasonably be expected of a person carrying on the particular director's duties, and the knowledge, skill and experience which the director actually possesses.[269] It is for the director to prove that he or she took every reasonable step to minimise potential losses. As noted in Chapter 3, this is a higher skill and care standard than is imposed on directors generally, where the test is based more on the actual qualities of the individual director, and less on the qualities which he or she ought reasonably to display.[270]

5.33 The effect of this formulation of the directors' duty is that honest but incompetent directors will not escape liability if they fail to foresee insolvency where a reasonable director would have foreseen it. Therefore, to discharge their duty when acting as stewards of a PSO, directors and committee members in industrial and provident societies need to ensure they remain aware of what is going on in the PSO, and review its finances regularly. Taking appropriate professional advice, if relevant to the PSO's situation, will also be important (even if this means spending the PSO's money to obtain the advice).

Potential liability

5.34 The potential consequence for appointees under the wrongful trading remedy will be to pay compensation to remedy the loss to creditors caused by their failure to act competently. The appointee is therefore potentially liable to the extent that the company was made worse off by their failure to appreciate the impending insolvency and minimise potential losses.[271] It is not intended to be punitive in nature.

---

[266] S.214. The provisions of this Act and the remedy of wrongful trading apply to appointees to industrial and provident societies: ss. 55(a), 56 Industrial and Provident Societies Act 1965 as amended; *Re Norse Self Build Association Ltd* [1985] BCLC 219 which confirmed that the court may wind up an industrial and provident society as if it were a registered company under the Insolvency Act 1986.

[267] Wrongful trading is considered a remedy rather than an offence because it is designed to compensate third parties who have suffered loss because of a director's incompetence, not to punish. There is a separate statutory offence of fraudulent trading: s.213 Insolvency Act 1986, which requires dishonesty to be proved.

[268] Section 214 Insolvency Act 1986. For detailed legal analysis on the section see Totty and Jordan *Insolvency* (looseleaf work) (FT Law & Tax) para B1.11; and for recent discussion of the elements of the remedy see M Hyde *Directors' Liability (3)* Solicitor's Journal 4 April 1997 307.

[269] S. 214 (4) *ibid.*

[270] It is this higher duty that, according to one judge, should form the test for the model director's duty of skill and care: see paragraph A28 ff above.

[271] *Re Produce Marketing Consortium Ltd (No 2)* [1989] 3 All ER 1; *Re Purpoint Ltd* [1991] BCLC 491.

5.35 The court does have discretion to award such compensation as it thinks proper.[272] However, it should be noted that one of the major forms of protection to be discussed in Chapter 6, namely the right of directors to claim relief from the court where a liability is imposed upon them when they have acted reasonably and honestly, is not available where the liability to be imposed is for wrongful trading.[273]

Application to other legal structures

5.36 The introduction of the remedy of wrongful trading for creditors of industrial and provident societies and companies and its higher standards have led to concerns that appointees to statutory or chartered corporations could also be liable to creditors of the PSO in the event of insolvency. As they are operating in an increasingly commercial (and contract-based) environment, appointees have questioned whether a court would apply the wrongful trading provisions to their conduct, in the event that a PSO ran out of funds, even though they possess a different legal structure.

5.37 Appendix D provides an analysis of the dissolution regimes for statutory and chartered corporations together with a discussion of the scope of the Insolvency Act 1986. It concludes that PSOs which are statutory or chartered corporations will not be construed as unregistered companies subject to the provisions of the Insolvency Act, and that the dissolution procedures for these two structures provide a complete system for dealing with the liabilities of these corporations.

Conclusions

5.38 To the extent that insolvency of a PSO is caused by an appointee's failure to fulfil their skill and care, fiduciary or governance responsibilities described in Chapter 4, appointees can be liable to the PSO for the consequences of that failure. However, where insolvency arises and appointees have not failed in this manner, there is no extra duty rendering them liable to the PSO itself.

5.39 As far as claims by creditors are concerned, there is an important difference between companies and industrial and provident societies on the one hand and statutory and chartered corporations on the other: creditors of the former have readily exercisable rights to secure their debts (which includes the right to obtain compensation from appointees in the liquidation process under wrongful trading provisions), while creditors of the latter have no equivalent rights. Therefore, appointees in companies and industrial and provident societies need to be aware of the additional requirements placed upon them, notwithstanding their limited liability status.

5.40 Appointees in non-corporate structures are at risk of personal liability to third parties when a PSO becomes insolvent since they are already acting in place of the PSO, and in this situation, the indemnity protection which they would otherwise enjoy will be worthless.

---

[272] s.214 (1) *ibid.*

[273] See *Re Produce Marketing op cit*, which held that section 727 of the Companies Act 1985 is not available to directors, since section 214 requires an objective assessment of the director's conduct, whereas section 727 is concerned with a subjective assessment. See Bradgate and Howells *No Excuse for Wrongful Trading* Journal of Business Law 1990 (May) 249–254 for a critique of this judgment which suggests that Knox J's reasoning is questionable, but that the result was correct. Section 727 is not available to appointees to industrial and provident societies in any event, since the provision applies only to true companies.

Chapter 6 – Protection from liability

Introduction

6.1 Chapters 4 and 5 have described the duties and responsibilities which are placed upon appointees when they serve on the responsible body of a PSO. They also set out the potential liability which can arise where appointees fail to perform a duty or responsibility properly. This chapter is concerned with the legal protection which is presently available to appointees to help them avoid incurring a potential liability.

6.2 Such protection can be divided into two classes:

(a) **Protection which prevents a liability occurring; and**

(b) **Protection which alleviates the consequences of a liability which an appointee is legally obliged to meet.**

6.3 The chapter shows that not all appointees can avail themselves equally of both classes of protection, and that there are weaknesses in the way protection is conferred on some appointees.

6.4 The particular form of protection conferred by 'limited liability', available to appointees in PSOs with corporate structures, has already been discussed in Chapters 3 and 5.

Overview

6.5 The principle which underpins both classes of protection is that appointees should not suffer personal liability where there has been no wrongdoing or act of bad faith on their part. As has been noted in the preceding two chapters, appointees are sometimes, exceptionally, at risk of potential liability even where they have been acting in the best interests of the PSO and in good faith.

6.6 For the most part, the law will only impose a potential liability where appointees have acted in a manner which deserves such imposition; i.e. where they have knowingly acted wrongfully, or deliberately ignored professional advice. For example, deliberately misappropriating the PSO's assets, or acting recklessly against advice when investing a PSO's funds, have been shown to be types of behaviour which will leave an appointee personally responsible for the adverse consequences. The types of protection discussed in this chapter are not intended to protect appointees in these circumstances.

6.7 However, potential liability can also arise where appointees have failed to understand the duties placed upon them; or where the law specifies that an appointee has failed to perform a particular duty without having acted wrongfully or in bad faith (e.g. the 'technical breach' problem discussed in Chapter 4). An example of the former will occur where an appointee fails to appreciate (and hence comply with) the strict legal rules forbidding personal benefit which operate in most PSOs, which can include much more than simple financial payments. However, with considerable guidance available to appointees on such matters, it is increasingly difficult for appointees to fail to fulfil the governing instruments' requirements by accident.

6.8 The latter situation, while relatively uncommon, can occur in relation to the fiduciary responsibilities and governance responsibilities described above. For example, acting without the proper authority of the responsible body can render some appointees personally liable to a third party for any loss caused thereby (under a breach of warranty of authority claim). As already shown, this liability can arise even where the appointee acted honestly, or the mistake was excusable.

6.9 Protection from liability is therefore important to appointees, and should not be seen as a means of excusing appointees for their wrongdoing. Moreover, since it is impossible to provide categoric reassurance for appointees on the subject of personal liability (particularly when every case turns on its facts), the availability of protection can help ensure that people are not discouraged from serving as appointees.

6.10 Before considering the different forms of protection, the question of limitation periods needs to be considered briefly.

Limitation periods

6.11 The rules on limitation provide time limits within which legal actions must be brought or else they become time-barred (i.e. they lapse). For many legal claims there is a period of 6 years from the date of its cause in which to bring an action, but this can be reduced, for example, to 1 year, or there may be no limit at all.[274]

6.12 In discussing the forms of protection available to appointees the text which follows does not discuss these rules on limitation. Although where the rules operate they will in effect shield appointees from the consequences of their conduct, they should not be seen as a true form of protection which can be invoked by appointees; rather they are provided to ensure claims are brought promptly and pursued diligently. They are not based on any qualitative judgement of an appointee's conduct, and will only be relevant if a legal action has not been brought for a matter of years after the event. For this reason, no further mention is made of limitation periods as a form of protection for appointees.[275]

Section A: preventing a potential liability occurring

Introduction

6.13 There are five ways at law in which protection can be afforded to an appointee to prevent a potential liability arising:

- (a) Statutory forms of relief;
- (b) Statutory forms of immunity;
- (c) Exclusion clauses;
- (d) Ratification of acts; and
- (e) Permission to bring proceedings.

6.14 The first two are important forms of protection which are provided by statute for appointees in certain types of legal structure. The remaining types may be used by appointees, PSOs, or their regulators on a case by case basis to prevent a potential liability materialising.

6.15 Table 2 below summarises the use which different legal structures of PSO can make of the five different types of protection. Each will then be described in turn, together with the problems which appointees may encounter with their use.

---

[274] E.g. for defamation claims the limit is now primarily 1 year following the Defamation Act 1996 (s.5), while if a claim relating to a trust involves fraud there may be no limitation period. See Limitation Act 1980, ss 2, 4A, 21. See also *Att-Gen v Cocke* [1985] Ch 414 suggesting that claims against trustees personally if brought by the Attorney General are not subject to limitation provisions.

[275] See the Limitation Act 1980 and *Limitation Periods* McGee (2nd ed 1994) for further details of the law in this respect.

Table 2

Legal structure	Statutory relief	Statutory immunity	Exclusion clauses[1]	Ratification of acts	Discretion to bring proceedings
Unincorporated associations	No	No	Yes	Yes	Yes[2]
Trusts	Yes	No	Yes	No	Yes[2]
Companies	Yes	No	No	Yes	Yes[2]
Statutory corporations	No	Some[3]	In theory	Yes	n/a
Chartered corporations	No	No	In theory	Yes	n/a
Industrial and provident societies	No	No	Yes	Yes	n/a

[1] Exclusion clauses can be used in governing instruments and in contracts or other transaction documents.

[2] If a registered charity.

[3] I.e. local authority schools and NHS trusts.

(a) Statutory forms of relief

6.16 Two types of appointee enjoy specific statutory provisions which give courts a power to relieve an appointee from potential liability in certain circumstances: namely, directors and trustees.[276]

6.17 Where directors or trustees have acted honestly and reasonably and ought fairly to be excused in all the circumstances, the court may order that they be excused from liability. This form of relief is not available for all potential liabilities incurred by a trustee or director, but it represents a significant safeguard.

6.18 For trustees, the protection will be available for claims which are a 'breach of trust'. This covers the skill and care, fiduciary and governance duties described in Chapter 4. However, it does not cover claims which third parties may bring against trustees, for example for breach of a contract which a trustee has entered into in place of the PSO.

6.19 For directors the relief is available for claims in negligence, default, breach of duty or breach of trust.[277] However, as with trustees, the relief applies only to actions brought by or on behalf of the PSO against the director (i.e. for breach of responsibilities owed to the PSO), and not for actions by third parties for breaches of a duty owed to them.[278]

6.20 It should be stressed that these are discretionary forms of relief, and appointees will be required to demonstrate to the court's satisfaction that they have fulfilled the criteria for being excused liability.

6.21 Few modern cases exist, and those that do tend to relate to the work of professional trustees (e.g. solicitors) or directors of commercial organisations. Indeed, every case will be judged on its particular facts and the courts have been reluctant to lay down general principles.[279]

---

[276] Directors: s.727 Companies Act 1985; Trustees: s.61 Trustee Act 1925.

[277] S.727 (1) Companies Act 1985.

[278] See *Customs & Excise Commrs v Hedon Alpha Ltd* [1981] QB 818. In *Re Produce Marketing Consortium* [1989] 3 All ER 1 it was held that s.727 relief was incompatible with the wrongful trading provisions of the Insolvency Act 1986, such that if liability for wrongful trading was proved, s.727 could not be invoked.

[279] *Re Turner* [1897] 1 Ch 536.

6.22 However, to cite some particular examples of the courts' use of these provisions, it has been held that a trustee who had done nothing and accepted without question the acts of co-trustees, was not entitled to relief.[280] But the act in question may be more than an administrative blunder and still attract relief; and relief may be granted where liability arises from an *ultra vires* act (e.g. where monies were paid in breach of the trust's governing instruments, on the erroneous advice of a solicitor[281]); relief has also been given to directors for *ultra vires* acts.[282]

6.23 Honesty alone on the part of the appointee is not sufficient. An appointee must also have acted reasonably (i.e. acting with such prudence as a person of ordinary intelligence and diligence might reasonably be expected to display in the conduct of their own affairs). Further, the court must agree that the trustee or director ought fairly to be excused (fair to the trustee or director, and anyone else involved).[283]

Application to other legal structures

6.24 Unincorporated associations, industrial and provident societies, chartered and statutory corporations do not have any specific statutory provision which provides the courts with an equivalent right to relieve.[284]

6.25 However, given the development of the 'quasi-trustee' described in Chapter 4, the question arises as to whether appointees who are treated like trustees can avail themselves of this protection even though they are not true trustees. The answer is unclear, and will remain so until there is a case testing the point.

6.26 The starting point of any analysis is that the Trustee Act 1925 can apply only to true trustees.[285] However, as noted earlier, appointees in registered charities (whether they are trusts, unincorporated associations or charitable companies) are defined as 'trustees' in the Charities Act 1993.[286] A court could decide that if an appointee is made subject to true trustee duties and standards, and taking into account the Charities Act definition, then the protection conferred by the Trustee Act 1925 should also apply. The difficulty with this argument is that the Charities Act 1993 is a discrete regime, intended to regulate the Charity Commission's work in relation to charities. Thus, the definitions included in the Charities Act are not intended to have effect in relation to the interpretation of other legislation.

6.27 Another possibility is that a court could exercise its inherent equitable jurisdiction (from which fiduciary duties are derived), and excuse an appointee on the grounds that they have acted honestly and in good faith, without being specifically covered by a statutory provision. In this analysis trustees and directors remain the exclusive beneficiaries of the statutory provisions, but the courts would provide equivalent relief to appointees who are treated like a trustee (or a director).

6.28 At present, however, it cannot be said with any certainty that a 'quasi-trustee' will enjoy this type of protection.

---

[280] *Re Second East Dulwich Building Society* (1899) 68 LJ Ch 196.

[281] See *Re Alsop, Whitaker v Bamford* [1914] 1 Ch 1 and the commentary on section 61 in *Halsbury's Statutes* 4th ed (1995 reissue) vol 48, p 334.

[282] *Re Claridges Patent Asphalte* [1921] 1 Ch 543.

[283] See, for example, *Re Turner, Barker v Ivimey* [1897] 1 Ch 536, and *Marsden v Regan* [1954] 1 All ER 475. Section 61 Trustee Act 1925 provides that the trustee ought to be fairly excused not just for the breach, but also for the failure of the trustee to obtain directions from the court before taking the said action. This is a right open to trustees where they are in doubt about the legality of their proposed conduct.

[284] There is no evidence that appointees in industrial and provident societies enjoy the protection of the Companies Act 1985 in this respect, notwithstanding the application of the insolvency regime described in Chapter 5 above.

[285] S.68 (1)(17) of the Act does not provide a comprehensive definition of 'trust' and 'trustee', and it will be a matter of construction of the facts of each case whether there is a 'trust' to which the Act will apply.

[286] S.97 (1) defines 'charity trustees' as the persons having the general control and management of the administration of a charity, and s.96 (1) defines 'charity' as any institution, corporate or not, which is established for charitable purposes, and is subject to the control of the High Court in the exercise of the court's jurisdiction with respect to charities.

Conclusions

6.29 Statutory forms of relief provide significant reassurance for appointees, which is important given the fact that personal liability will always depend on the facts of a particular case. Although it is limited to certain types of claim, it represents a genuine form of protection for those rare cases where appointees face potential liability but are guilty of no wrongdoing. It is, however, only available to two types of appointee at present.

(b) Statutory forms of immunity

6.30 Another form of protection offered to some, but by no means most appointees, is statutory immunity. This is where a statute specifically prevents a claim of a certain type being brought against an appointee; they are made 'immune from suit'. This form of protection is rare, but two examples are relevant to PSOs.

6.31 Local authority school governors have a form of immunity relating to their use of the local authority's delegated school budget, provided they have acted in good faith;[287] and NHS trust directors and nominee appointees from local authorities have a degree of immunity conferred on them by the Public Health Act 1875, provided they also have acted in good faith.[288]

6.32 The standard of conduct required in order to qualify for immunity is expressed differently to the statutory forms of relief discussed above. Instead of an 'honestly and reasonably' requirement, the test is acting 'in good faith'. The real difference between these is the fact that while good faith requires honesty on the part of the appointee, it does not necessarily require reasonableness. Thus, the test for statutory relief appears to offer a more objective test than that for conferring the statutory immunity.

6.33 There is no case law on the school governors' immunity provision, which is a relatively recent development.[289] It is designed to protect school governors when they take decisions about how to spend the school budget. As they are doing so as agents of the local authority, there is the potential for a 'surcharge' claim to be made in the event that they make a payment 'contrary to law' or cause a loss to the local authority by 'wilful misconduct'.[290] Therefore the immunity provision provides additional comfort for governors, to protect them against surcharge liability.[291]

6.34 Contractual liability is unlikely to be an issue for governors since the school will be entering into contracts using the legal personality of the responsible body (which is a statutory corporation). However, the statutory provision confers immunity on school governors for any other claim in relation to their use of the budget for the purposes of the school, provided they have acted in good faith, which will always be a question of fact. It should be noted, however, that it will be difficult to breach the fiduciary or governance duties outlined above, and still keep within the ambit of this immunity, since both are essentially duties of good faith.

---

[287] Under the Local Management in Schools regime: Education Act 1996 Part II, Chapter V, s.116 (8) (consolidating section 36 (6) of the Education Reform Act 1988): "The governors of a school shall not incur any personal liability in respect of anything done in good faith in the exercise or purported exercise of their powers under subsection (5)." Subsection (5) refers to the governing body's powers to spend the school budget delegated from the local authority "as they think fit". The immunity does not apply to grant maintained school governors who have no such delegated budget, receiving their funds from central government instead.

[288] Originally intended for local authority members and officers, section 265 of the Public Health Act 1875 states: "[N]o matter or thing done by any member of any [local] authority or by any officer of such authority or other person whomsoever acting up at the direction of such authority shall, if the matter or thing were done ... bona fide for the purpose of executing this Act, or any other public general Act, subject them or any of them personally to any action liability claim or demand whatsoever". The section applies to NHS trusts by virtue of section 125 of the National Health Service Act 1977, and Schedule 2, paragraph 25 of the National Health Service and Community Care Act 1990 and non-executive directors constitute 'officers' within the meaning of the section. The section also contains an indemnity, which is discussed at paragraph 6.107 below.

[289] Its origin was the Education Reform Act 1988.

[290] See ss. 19 and 20 of the Local Government Finance Act (LGFA) 1982 respectively.

[291] S.116 (8) is in addition to the defence that already exists under the LGFA 1982 for 'contrary to law' claims, to the effect that no surcharge liability will arise if the court is satisfied that the governor acted reasonably or in the belief that the expenditure was authorised by law (s.19 (3)).

6.35 No other PSOs in the education world or other sectors enjoy similar immunity, and it is the unique relationship between local authorities and their schools which gives rise to it.[292]

6.36 The scope of the statutory immunity which applies to NHS trust directors and to local authority nominee appointees is not entirely clear.[293] The confusion arises from attempts by the corporate bodies themselves (e.g. the health board or the local authority) to invoke the immunity. Such attempts have usually failed, but the case law has developed somewhat haphazardly.

6.37 It has been held that the words 'and without negligence' should be read into the provision, so that it is necessary to have acted in good faith and without negligence before the immunity will operate: *Bullard v Croydon Health Group Management Committee*.[294] This case was concerned with the act of a management committee, and not the individuals who served on it,[295] and therefore may be distinguished from cases involving individual appointees. However, in a more recent case, involving council officers nominated to serve on an outside body, the judge followed the *Bullard* reasoning, and held that the acts of the officers had to be both *bona fide* and without negligence to bring them within the scope of the section.[296]

6.38 If this view of the law is correct, the immunity conferred in section 265 is more limited than it appears on its face. Negligence and good faith are not mutually exclusive – it would be possible for an appointee to have acted negligently (e.g. by failing to take adequate care to check that there was proper authority to act) but nonetheless acted in good faith (i.e. it was an honest mistake). If the want of care was particularly reckless, then it probably would not be judged in good faith. However, there is less protection conferred upon appointees if the act must also be without negligence.

6.39 It is unlikely that the section will provide immunity for *ultra vires* acts for these classes of appointee,[297] or for contract claims,[298] or criminal prosecutions;[299] and (as with school governors) since the acts must be bona fide it may be difficult to invoke the immunity where breaches of the fiduciary and governance duties are involved.

---

[292] Prior to the 1992 reforms which saw further education institutions separated from local authority management and funding, there was a similar statutory immunity for the appointees to these institutions, where they spent the local authority budget. Following the creation of the further education corporations this was repealed – see s.142 (7) Education Reform Act 1988.

[293] Although the original immunity is conferred in an Act relating to public health, section 39 of the Local Government (Miscellaneous Provisions) Act 1976 extends the protection more generally to local authority officers. Nominee appointees from local authorities may derive protection from section 265 to the extent that the acts giving rise to the potential liability are for the purposes of the local authority, and within its powers. Thus, the immunity extends beyond public health matters to legitimate local authority matters for local authority appointees.

[294] [1953] 1 QBD 511.

[295] There is doubt over the extent to which the immunity can be invoked by corporate bodies, e.g. a local authority or NHS trust, as opposed to the individuals who serve it. In *Southampton and Itchen Bridge Co v Local Bd of Southampton* [1858] 8 E & B 801 it was held that the Board of Southampton itself could not benefit from the protection afforded by an equivalent provision to s.265. It is probably the case that section 265 is not intended to protect the corporate body, and is intended only for the individuals who serve it; under this analysis the purpose of the section is to ensure claims are brought against the proper parties (e.g. the corporate body rather than the individual, unless the individual was guilty of bad faith), and not to bar a third party's remedies altogether, which would be its effect otherwise.

[296] See *Burgoine and Cooke v London Borough of Waltham Forest and McWhirr* The Times 7 November 1996, Neuberger J (pp38–40 transcript). The officers sought to rely on the indemnity part of the section rather than the immunity part, but this part of the reasoning is unaffected by the distinction. The case arose out of a wrongful trading liability imposed on the officers.

[297] The section is drafted to cover the acts of officers carried out for the purposes of the particular legislation referred to: in the case of local authorities, the local government acts establishing their powers, and in the case of NHS trusts, the National Health Service and Community Care Act 1990. These Acts confer wide powers on both bodies, but if the act is outside the governing instruments it is probably not protected. See also the dicta of Neuberger J in *Burgoine op cit*. Note, however, that in the case of local authority nominees, it is whether the act is *ultra vires* the local authority's powers that is relevant, rather than *ultra vires* the PSO to which the appointee is nominated.

[298] The section is intended to provide immunity for acts relating to the exercise of powers under the given legislation (what one commentator refers to as the "public duties": see *Speller's Law of Hospitals* (1994) p49), rather than the commercial dealings of the corporate body. It is unlikely, in any event, that individual appointees will be signing contracts for corporate bodies, unless the local authority nominee is serving in a trust or unincorporated association on behalf of the local authority.

[299] The statutory wording of any "action, liability, claim or demand" would not seem to include criminal prosecutions.

Conclusions

6.40 Statutory forms of immunity are rare and are not generally favoured by English courts, hence the attempts to whittle away the protection afforded by them, as described above. Given the judicial interpretation of section 265, it remains to be seen whether the courts would treat the immunity conferred on school governors in a similar manner and introduce the requirement that the acts of the appointee be without negligence.

6.41 As an alternative to the statutory forms of relief, statutory immunity has the potential to confer significant protection on appointees. However, the attitude of the courts to the existing provisions suggests that affording courts discretion to relieve is a more acceptable and certain method of providing protection for appointees.

(c) Exclusion clauses

6.42 While the two types of protection discussed above are provided by statute, exclusion clauses are a means of protection which can be used on a case by case basis by appointees and PSOs. They can be used in governing instruments to specify that appointees will not be liable for certain acts, *where the act would breach a duty to the PSO*. In some circumstances they can also be used in dealings with third parties to limit liability. However, the type of liability that can be the subject of the exclusion is regulated by both statute law and the regulators responsible for different types of PSO.

6.43 Such clauses can limit or reduce the duties which the appointee would otherwise owe to the PSO, or they can expressly restrict the appointee's liability for a breach of duty. The result, in both cases, is the same: the potential liability will not materialise.

Excluding liability to the PSO

6.44 Unincorporated associations may (and frequently do) use their governing instruments (which are a form of contract between the members) to limit or exclude liability as between members. Trust deeds may also limit a trustee's liability for acts which are in breach of trust, for example by stating that liability will only arise if the trustee has acted dishonestly.[300] There is no statutory limit on how widely such clauses are drafted.

6.45 Companies, on the other hand, are prevented by statute from including in their governing instruments any provision which seeks to exempt a director from liability which the law might attach for "negligence, default, breach of duty or breach of trust".[301] This means that exclusion clauses will not be available to prevent a director being liable for breach of many of the duties described in Chapter 4.[302]

6.46 No examples of exclusion clauses have been identified in the governing instruments of the statutory corporations or the chartered corporations studied, although, at law, there is no reason why they should not exist. Industrial and provident societies can put such clauses in their rules, and registered social landlords often include a clause exempting liability for appointees except for losses caused by dishonesty or gross negligence.

Excluding liability to third parties

6.47 Exclusion clauses can also be used in transactions with third parties, to limit liability. They are generally unnecessary for PSOs with corporate structures, but where non-corporate appointees are concluding contracts in place of their PSO, they may include terms in the agreement to limit any potential liability to the assets of the PSO.

---

[300] In the recent case of *Armitage v Nurse* The Times 31 March 1997, the Court of Appeal held that an exemption clause in a trust deed could validly exclude liability for 'gross negligence', rejecting arguments that such a clause was repugnant or contrary to public policy. For further discussion of this case see Panesar *Actual Fraud and Gross Negligence: The Scope of Trustee Exemption Clauses* Business Law Review Jan 1998 vol 19 pp8–14.

[301] See s.310 Companies Act 1985.

[302] The *quid pro quo* of this is the provision of limited indemnities and full insurance for directors in the governing instruments, for which see further below.

The potential liability might be for breach of contract, or for an act of negligence. Such clauses will be of assistance to the appointee if the PSO becomes insolvent, for reasons set out at paragraph 6.104 below. However, it is often difficult to persuade the other party to the contract to include such provisions.

6.48 There is significant statutory intervention in the field of exclusion clauses. The most important provisions are contained in the Unfair Contracts Terms Act 1977, which regulate exclusion clauses in contracts concerned with a business liability and in many cases where one party is dealing as a consumer.[303] A business liability is defined as including the activities of a government department or public or local authority, and the business need not be carried on for profit.[304] Where appointees are undertaking activities which fall within the Act's ambit, they are unable to exclude liability for death and personal injury caused by their negligence, and in some cases clauses concerning contractual liability will have to be 'reasonable' before they can take effect.[305] There are also statutory rules concerning the ability to limit liability to other people for misrepresentations.[306]

6.49 The statutory limitations described in the preceding paragraph do not affect any exclusion terms included in governing instruments by PSOs as described above.[307]

Conclusions

6.50 Exclusion clauses can be useful for appointees in non-corporate structures to overcome the problems which a lack of legal identity poses for them. Used on a case by case basis they can

provide reassurance about the extent of the personal liabilities which appointees can incur when they act for the PSO.

(d) Ratification

6.51 Like exclusion clauses, ratification allows PSOs to absolve appointees of personal liability on a case by case basis.

6.52 In Chapter 4, the position of appointees who act without authority was discussed, and it was noted that potential liability could arise because the PSO did not sanction the acts of the appointee.[308] The consequences of such unauthorised acts could lead to a potential liability to the PSO, or to third parties. However, it is possible for some PSOs to ratify the acts of appointees after the event, so that the potential breach of duty is removed. If this happens the PSO legally adopts the appointee's act, rendering an action by the PSO or a claim by a third party against the appointee impossible or redundant, since the PSO will have agreed to assume whatever unauthorised act the appointee has undertaken. Ratification may be used only where it is in its corporate interest to do so.

6.53 This form of protection can be of particular importance where appointees have made honest mistakes, such as acting without proper authority, without any wrongdoing on their part. As already shown in Chapter 4, without such ratification a breach of warranty of authority claim could arise.

6.54 The acts which can be ratified are breaches of the fiduciary or governance duties, and, in theory, the skill and care duty, all of which may or may not

---

[303] See *Chitty on Contracts* (27th ed 1994) chap 14 for detailed discussion of the law on exemption clauses in contracts, and the statutory limitations. In relation to consumer transactions, see also Directive 93/13/EEC on Unfair Terms in Consumer Contracts and the UK Regulations derived therefrom.

[304] S.14 and *Roles v Miller* (1884) 27 Ch D 71, 88; *Town Investments Ltd v Dept of Environment* [1978] AC 359.

[305] Unfair Contract Terms Act 1977, ss. 2,3.

[306] S.3 Misrepresentation Act 1967, as amended.

[307] See paragraph 1, Schedule 1 to the Unfair Contract Terms Act 1977. Contracts relating to the formation or dissolution of a company, including an unincorporated association, or relating to its constitution or the rights or obligations of its members are not subject to these restrictions.

[308] See paragraphs A100 ff above.

involve potential liability to third parties, as well as the PSO itself. However, it would need to be established how any ratification of the breach of a skill and care duty was in the interests of the PSO itself, before it could be permitted. As discussed in Chapter 4, there is a difference between an act which the PSO could legally have authorised, but which, in fact, it did not, and an act which was altogether outside the PSO's powers. Ratification is easier to achieve in the first of these instances than in the second.

6.55 The rules governing ratification can be somewhat technical in nature. Taking companies first, a company has always been able to ratify, by ordinary resolution, acts which are beyond a director's authority (but which are within the powers of the company), or breaches of fiduciary duties.[309] Following the company law reforms of 1989, companies can also ratify acts which are truly *ultra vires* the company, but this time by special resolution. These ratifications have the effect of adopting the particular act. To relieve the director of liability for participating in the unauthorised act, a separate special resolution must also be passed.[310]

6.56 For charitable companies which wish to ratify acts of directors in breach of their duties because they are unauthorised or *ultra vires*, the prior written permission of the Charity Commission must first be obtained.[311]

6.57 Unincorporated associations, industrial and provident societies, and chartered and statutory corporations can also use ratification to adopt the acts of appointees, and authorise their

unauthorised conduct. However, this will only be possible if the acts were within the powers of the PSO's governing instruments in the first place. This is because, unlike companies, these structures do not have equivalent statutory provisions validating *ultra vires* acts. Thus, the act which is outside the PSO's powers is void, and cannot be adopted (without changing the terms of the governing instruments[312]); whereas the act which was simply unauthorised can be ratified subsequently, by the members of the PSO.[313]

6.58 The concept of ratification is not applicable to trusts.

Conclusions

6.59 Ratification is extremely useful for appointees since it allows PSOs to remove potential liability from them, where they have acted honestly and with the best of intentions. In particular it can assist appointees where a technical failure to comply with the fiduciary or governance duties is involved.

(e) Permission to bring proceedings

6.60 Reference has been made in Chapters 4 and 5 to the identity of the people who are able to bring proceedings against an appointee for breach of a duty. Where there is a breach of duty to the PSO, the PSO, as represented by the responsible body or the members, can take action. Where a third party is involved they too may have rights against the appointee. However, for one group of PSOs the permission of third parties must be sought before particular actions can be brought against appointees: namely registered charities.[314]

---

[309] In an ordinary meeting of the members of the company – who will be defined in the governing instruments. See *Bamford v Bamford* [1970] Ch 212.

[310] S.35 (3) Companies Act 1985, as amended. Commentators have noted that the double resolution procedure is peculiar given that such acts are already binding upon the company, as a result of s.35 (1).

[311] Charities Act 1993 s.65 (4).

[312] This might be technically possible, but the permission of the Charity Commission would be needed for any registered charity, and the agreement of the relevant government department or regulator for chartered and statutory corporations, and industrial and provident societies.

[313] This distinction may not actually increase the liability of appointees, given the fact that if the act could not have been performed by the PSO in any event no breach of warranty claim will necessarily arise; see the discussion at paragraph A109 ff above.

[314] But note, not exempt charities – for which see Appendix A.

6.61 The position is that before 'charity proceedings' can be brought by or against a charity or its appointees, the permission of the Charity Commission must be obtained, or if that is refused, that of the High Court.[315] The definition of 'charity proceedings' includes any action against an appointee for breach of their duties to the charity,[316] but does not include actions to enforce common law or contractual rights, or relator actions.[317] Further, proceedings may only be brought by specified persons, namely, the charity itself (if incorporated), one or more charity appointees, two or more inhabitants of the area if it is a 'local charity', or a person interested in the charity.[318] This last class of person is not capable of easy definition – the courts have shied away from giving a definitive test. However, a person whose financial contributions give them rights in the administration of the charity qualifies, but making a one-off donation, having a contract with the appointees or being a potential beneficiary of the charity probably do not.[319]

6.62 In considering whether to grant permission, the Commissioners have to consider whether the matter would be better dealt with under their statutory powers. The requirement for permission means that vexatious or frivolous claims should be prevented, but the Commissioners will not be acting as a court of first instance in deciding whether to grant permission. Thus, this type of protection while acting as a form of filter, is not equivalent to the previous methods described above.

6.63 It should also be pointed out that, while no formal steps such as described above are needed to commence actions against appointees in other legal structures, where it is a duty to the PSO which an appointee fails to fulfil, the PSO (or a member) will need to agree that action for that breach should be taken against the erring appointee. Thus, there is always some sort of discretion to bring proceedings, even when not laid down in statute.

Conclusions

6.64 Requiring permission to bring charity proceedings provides a filtration process that assists appointees to avoid vexatious or frivolous claims. While not complete in its protection, because it does not cover certain types of claims, it should be of reassurance to appointees in registered charities.

---

[315] S.33 Charities Act 1993. The language of the act is concerned with 'trustees', which covers appointees to unincorporated associations and charitable companies, as well as true trusts.

[316] S.33(8) *ibid.* Where the action is for an alleged breach of duty, the normal rule that all appointees must be joined in the action does not apply.

[317] Relator actions are actions brought by the Attorney General, on behalf of individuals, to assert a public right. However, such actions are now seldom used.

[318] S.33(1) *ibid.* The Attorney General has separate powers to bring proceedings against appointees who have failed in their duties, as does the Charity Commission of its own volition (provided the Attorney agrees), following recent reforms: s.32 *ibid.*

[319] See *Tudor on Charities* (8th ed 1995) p344 ff, and the cases cited therein.

Section B: relief from consequences of liability

Introduction

6.65 Even if appointees are not able to rely on one of the forms of protection described in Section A above, meaning that a liability is imposed upon them, this is not the end of the story. The other class of legal relief available to appointees operates by relieving them from the consequences of a liability.

6.66 There are two ways in law that this can happen:[320]

    (a) Insurance; and

    (b) Indemnities.

6.67 These two types of protection are intended to remove the costs to the appointee of bearing a liability where there has been no deliberate wrongdoing or act of bad faith. They cannot remove the fact that the appointee is rendered liable in the eyes of the law, but they can alleviate the financial consequences.

6.68 The governing instruments of the PSO are particularly relevant to these forms of protection.

(a) Insurance

6.69 In discussing when insurance will be available to protect appointees, three different questions need to be considered:

    (i) Whether a PSO can purchase insurance from its own funds to cover appointees for a personal liability;

    (ii) If it can, what type and scope of behaviour will be protected; and

    (iii) Whether the cost of insurance is appropriate in relation to the risks which are being insured.

6.70 The last of these is not a legal question, but is touched upon in the discussion which follows.

(i) Can a PSO purchase insurance from its own funds?

6.71 Not every PSO can acquire personal liability insurance from its own funds for the benefit of its appointees.[321]

6.72 A PSO's governing instruments need expressly to sanction the purchase of this type of insurance, because the fiduciary duty stating that appointees must not personally benefit from their position would otherwise prevent an appointee from lawfully taking the benefit of such a policy.[322]

6.73 The situation varies for the different types of PSOs studied, as set out in Table 3 below.

6.74 As will be seen, there is no consistency in the attitude taken to the purchase of personal liability insurance.

6.75 Until recently, the Charity Commission did not agree to registered charities purchasing personal liability insurance for appointees. However, this rule has been relaxed for the many PSOs which it regulates, and charities will not be prevented from registering if such insurance is made available to appointees.[323]

6.76 The regulators which oversee the various statutory corporations studied (e.g. the funding councils for further education colleges and grant maintained

---

[320] Contribution rights, discussed at paragraph 4.10 above, could constitute a third form of this type of protection. They do not release an appointee from total liability, but they provide a legal means for the liability to be shared amongst all those responsible.

[321] Personal liability insurance is also known as 'trustee liability insurance' or 'directors and officers (D&O) insurance'. It has two elements to it: a policy which indemnifies appointees themselves against liabilities and costs incurred in defending claims made against them for wrongful acts; and a policy which indemnifies the PSO in the event that it has to recompense the appointee for a personal liability. Although both produce the same result, the study is concerned with the first of these.

[322] See paragraph A63 ff above.

[323] The Charity Commission will also agree to the addition of a clause allowing such insurance, in 'appropriate cases'. In every case the PSO will have to justify its need for insurance. See Charity Commission Guide CC49 *Charities and Insurance* (June 1996). In particular charitable companies are not in the same position as companies, and require the Commission's consent notwithstanding the provisions of s.310(3) of the Companies Act 1985.

Table 3

PSO	Insurance obtainable[1]	Legal notes
NHS trusts	NO	Treasury requirements prevent NHS trusts from purchasing personal liability insurance: see *Government Accounting* and details below.
FE colleges	YES	Permitted by governing instruments (para 10(4) SI 1992/1963) and Further Education Funding Councils for England and for Wales.
Pre-1992 universities Post-1992 universities	YES	Paragraph 4.19 of the *CUC Guide*[2] states that it is "desirable for governing bodies to take out insurance against costs of any claims of negligence which may be made against members ... in carrying out their duties".
Grant maintained schools	NO	GM schools are required to purchase insurance for employer's and public liability risks for the protection of the responsible body, but no provision is made for the school's funds to be spent on personal liability insurance.
Local authority maintained schools	NO	The funds of local authority schools are delegated to be spent for the *purposes* of the school. The purchase of such insurance would be an unlawful use of the school budget (being a personal benefit not permitted by the governing instruments), and the local authority could not reimburse separately.
NDPBs	NO	The rules of *Government Accounting*, and the Financial Memorandum between each NDPB and its host department prevent the purchase of personal liability insurance. See further below.
Registered charities	YES	Provided the governing instruments contain an express term permitting the purchase, insurance can be provided from the charity's funds. The Charity Commission needs to approve any new term in the governing instruments.[3]
TECs	YES	Companies Act 1985 s.310 (3) (as amended) expressly allows for insurance to be purchased for a director's "negligence, default, breach of duty or breach of trust" in relation to the company. The DfEE/DTI TEC Licence makes it a requirement that such insurance is purchased (clause 5 1997 version).
Registered social landlords	POSSIBLY	Under the Housing Act 1996 Schedule 1: no personal benefit is to be received, other than limited remuneration and expenses. It is not clear whether insurance premiums represent an unlawful payment on this basis. The Housing Corporation has given no determination on this point.

1   I.e. personal liability insurance purchased from PSO's funds.

2   *Guide for Members of Governing Bodies of Universities and Colleges in England and Wales* Committee of University Chairmen/Higher Education Funding Councils for England and Wales (June 1995).

3   See Charity Commission Guide CC49 *Charities and Insurance* (June 1996) and *Decisions of the Charity Commissioners* volumes 2 and 4.

schools), and the government departments which established these bodies take differing views on the purchase of this type of insurance. For example, the former may acquire it, the latter may not, and nor may local authority maintained schools. The justification for the exclusion is the belief that appointees in these institutions run no risk of liability where they act in good faith, and that, therefore, public monies should not be spent on insurance.

6.77 In the case of executive non-departmental public bodies (NDPBs), insurance may not be purchased for appointees and instead they must rely on an indemnity from the Treasury and PSO for protection.[324] This results from the rules on the purchase of insurance by Crown bodies, contained in *Government Accounting*,[325] and the Treasury's interpretation thereof. NDPBs are expressly covered by the terms of these rules which will be mirrored in the funding agreements between departments and NDPBs.

6.78 Although *Government Accounting* itself does not forbid the purchase of insurance, it enunciates two reasons for purchasing a commercial insurance policy: (a) because there is a financial advantage to doing so since claims met are likely to exceed premiums paid; and (b) to protect the livelihood or businesses of the insured. Reason (b) is not considered relevant to government, since its business is so large (and its assets so great) that its viability is unaffected by potential claims. Therefore, to justify commercial insurance, reason (a) is the only relevant consideration.

6.79 The general presumption is that it will not be to the financial advantage of the Crown for commercial insurance to be purchased.[326] In the case of personal liability insurance for NDPB appointees the Treasury follows this line, and does not consent to its purchase by an NDPB from

funds derived from any source including the government grant. Reason (b) does not appear to have played a part in this decision, despite the fact that personal liability insurance, unlike all other types of insurance which the Crown may be purchasing, is concerned with the business or livelihood of an individual, and not with the Crown itself. The study has discovered no examples of NDPBs which have succeeded in making a case that they should be allowed to purchase commercial insurance to cover the risk of personal liability for their appointees.

6.80 Therefore, at present not all appointees covered by the study are able to purchase personal liability insurance using the PSO's funds. There is, of course, nothing to prevent appointees themselves purchasing this type of insurance for their activities in relation to a PSO. However, since the majority of appointees are not paid for their services, this option is not an attractive one.

(ii) Scope of protected behaviour

6.81 Where PSOs are able to purchase personal liability insurance, questions arise about the scope of behaviour that should be protected. The behaviour that could lead to personal liability ranges from honest mistakes or errors of judgement, through negligent or reckless acts to wilful or dishonest conduct. However, an insurance policy will not be able to protect an appointee from the consequences of all of these.

6.82 Under general principles of insurance law, PSOs will not be able to purchase insurance to cover the deliberate wrongdoing, fraud or criminal activities of appointees.[327] Nor would PSOs want to. However, there is nothing at law which prevents insurance being purchased to protect careless, unthinking or stupid behaviour.

---

[324] The problems which have arisen in relation to this indemnity are set out below at paragraph 6.116 ff.

[325] ISBN 0 11 560063 9, available from The Stationery Office, at chapter 27.

[326] There are limited exceptions to this (for which see chapter 27 *Government Accounting*).

[327] See the discussion in *MacGillivray on Insurance Law* 9th ed (1997) on illegality and insurance contracts, chap 14.

6.83 The personal liability policies used in the commercial world for company directors provide insurance protection for the 'wrongful acts' of directors. Each policy will then define precisely what is meant by the term 'wrongful act', but policies can and do cover acts and omissions which amount to a breach of trust, a breach of fiduciary duty, a want of skill or care, libel and slander, negligence, errors of judgement, misstatements and breach of warranty of authority (provided the 'wrongful act' relates to the activities of the organisation in question). Therefore, directors can obtain the benefit of very wide coverage.

6.84 Of these wrongful acts, the behaviour which has attracted the most comment is the cover provided for negligence. Negligence has a particular meaning at law, in relation to the duty of care, but in the insurance context it means no more than 'a want of care'; 'gross negligence' is a particularly grave want of care, and can also be termed 'gross recklessness'.[328] Some policies will cover negligence, but not gross negligence, leaving it a question of fact to be determined on each claim what the particular conduct amounted to. However, there is no difficulty in the insurance market about negligence (i.e. not taking sufficient care) being covered by an insurance policy.

6.85 Some, but by no means all, policies do describe certain conduct which is expressly excluded from being a 'wrongful act' under the policy (i.e. from being the subject of a claim). Fraudulent and deliberately wrongful acts or omissions are one example already mentioned.[329] Acts covered by other insurance policies will also be exempt.[330] It is also usual in policies which PSOs would purchase to remove cover for any claim relating to an unlawful benefit or profit received by an appointee. This means 'unlawful' under the governing instruments, as well as the general criminal law. Thus, if remuneration has been wrongly paid, or an unauthorised personal profit is made, insurance policies will tend not to cover any claim arising out of it.

6.86 In theory there is nothing to prevent companies obtaining insurance to protect against an order of compensation in a wrongful trading situation, although if the company is charitable, the approval of the Charity Commission will need to be sought.[331]

6.87 The policies which have been developed for registered charities closely resemble the policies just described for commercial organisations.[332] However, for registered charities there is an added requirement imposed by the Charity Commission that all policies purchased include a term as follows:

"The insurers shall not be liable for loss arising from any act or omission which the trustee knew to be a breach of trust or breach of duty or which was committed by the trustee in reckless disregard of whether it was a breach of trust or breach of duty or not."

6.88 Appointees to registered charities may therefore enjoy protection from personal liability for acts which were properly undertaken, or acts which were in breach of trust, but under an honest mistake. 'Reckless disregard' would seem close to gross negligence, and it is understood that, following the *Armitage v Nurse* case referred to at footnote 300 above, consideration is being given to the validity of this exclusion in the Charity Commission's standard clause.

---

[328] Gross negligence has found much judicial disfavour as a means of interpreting the duty of care owed at common law, but is still an accurate means of distinguishing a severe want of care from a mere mistake – see the discussion in *Charlesworth & Percy on Negligence* (9th ed 1997) on the meaning of negligence, pp 3 to 17.

[329] Although a requirement of general law, policies usually spell this out. Insurance policies will also not provide cover for loss arising from civil or criminal fines or penalties imposed by law, but will generally include loss arising from damages, judgments, settlements and defence costs.

[330] Personal liability policies are not intended to provide cover for personal injury, employer's liability or property damage claims since separate policies are available for these liabilities (and, indeed, required by law in many cases). Appointees need to be aware therefore (particularly in non-corporate structures) that more than one policy may be necessary to give protection. These policies are not viewed as personal protection for the appointee however, but as a concomitant of the PSO's activities, and are distinguished on this basis.

[331] This is because the compensation to be paid by the director probably equates to damages and not a fine – see footnote 329 above.

[332] Various policies developed for charities have been considered during the research.

Types of liability

6.89 Linked with the question of the scope of protected behaviour is the issue of whether insurance will cover all possible breaches of duty which an appointee can commit. Here, the distinction between liability to the PSO and liability to a third party is important. The liabilities owed to the PSO can be covered by insurance policies as described above.

6.90 However, the position differs for personal liabilities owed to third parties. In general it appears that as a matter of policy, insurance for ordinary contractual debts is not available in the insurance market. Therefore, appointees in trusts and unincorporated associations will not be covered under a personal liability policy for potential liability for claims under contracts they have entered into in place of the PSO.[333]

6.91 Equally, as noted above, a personal liability policy will not cover every type of claim which may befall a PSO. Public liability insurance, employer's liability insurance and property insurance are separate types of cover which may need to be purchased by PSOs, depending on their activities. For corporate PSOs these will be aimed at protecting the legal personality of the PSO. For non-corporate PSOs, they will protect the appointee in their role as employer, owner of property etc. Care needs to be taken therefore to understand the relationship between different policies.

Conclusions

6.92 There is no consistency in the attitude of PSOs, regulators and government departments on whether appointees should be permitted to receive the benefit of personal liability insurance from the PSO's funds.

6.93 Where appointees are able to obtain it, a very wide range of behaviour may be protected by the policy as a matter of law, although not deliberately wrongful acts.

6.94 In any discussion of insurance the issue of risks versus costs must be considered. It is important that the true risks of personal liability being run by appointees are assessed, before making a decision to purchase insurance. Much work has been undertaken in the charities field by organisations such as the National Council for Voluntary Organisations, to highlight the relatively low risks of personal liability for appointees, provided they understand their duties, and the relatively high premiums which can be charged. The need to justify the purchase of insurance is a constant theme in guidance offered to PSOs, particularly the need to assess the true risks which are being run.

6.95 Notwithstanding the need for caution in purchasing insurance, however, its availability is a significant comfort to appointees concerned about their position in an increasingly litigious society. While not an answer to the need for appointees to understand fully the duties placed upon them, insurance does represent a means of protecting appointees from liability which may arise without dishonesty or bad faith on their part.

(b) Indemnities

6.96 Indemnities are a form of guarantee for appointees that in the event that they are held personally liable they will be recompensed for whatever expense they have suffered. They are similar to insurance in terms of the outcome achieved. Indemnities can be offered to classes of appointee by statute and common law, and they may also be available on a case by case basis for individual appointees in a PSO's governing instruments.[334] In all cases the source of the funds from which the indemnity is to be paid needs to be identified.

---

[333] Note that section 61 Trustee Act 1925 will not provide any protection here either, so that exclusion clauses and indemnities are the only form of protection available for such appointees.

[334] The indemnity can also be set out in a separate contractual document. The important point is that the governing instruments must sanction the grant of any such indemnity.

Table 4

Legal structure	May indemnities be provided by the PSO?	May indemnities be provided by Third Parties?[1]	Are indemnities provided by statute?
Unincorporated associations	Yes	Yes	No
Trusts	Yes	Yes	Yes
Companies	Very limited	Yes	No
Statutory corporations	Yes[2]	Yes	Sometimes[3]
Chartered corporations	Yes[2]	Yes	No
Industrial and provident societies	No	Yes	No

[1]   For the particular position of nominee appointees see paragraphs 6.110 ff below.

[2]   But rarely used unless PSO is also an NDPB, since insurance is normally purchased.

[3]   For NHS trusts or local authority nominees.

6.97 Indemnities are particularly important where insurance is unavailable. Table 4 summarises the different uses which the various PSOs studied can make of indemnities.

6.98 Three particular areas are addressed below: the general availability of indemnities in corporate and non-corporate structures; indemnities that are available to nominee appointees; and PSOs which are obliged to use indemnities instead of insurance.

General availability: non-corporate structures

6.99 The indemnity is of vital importance to appointees in non-corporate structures. Since they are acting in place of their PSO in many circumstances, they are potentially liable in a number of situations where there has been no wrongdoing on their part. See Chapter 4 Section A for details.

6.100 Trustees have a right at common law to an indemnity from the funds of the trust to reimburse them for charges and expenses incurred in the execution of the trust.[335] This has received statutory support in the form of an express indemnity for trustees.[336]

6.101 The scope of the indemnity is that wherever trustees carry out activities within the terms of the governing instruments they are entitled to call upon the trust funds to reimburse them. Thus appointees can recover *payments* made for the purposes of the trust, and *liabilities* incurred for the purposes of the trust. In most cases these liabilities will be contractual, but there is no reason in theory why a liability in damages for a tort should not be covered by the indemnity, provided the trustee has not been personally at fault, e.g. has acted in accordance with the governing

---

[335]   *Worrall v Harford* (1802) 8 Ves 4.

[336]   S.30(2) Trustee Act 1925. Rights of subrogation and rights of lien also arise as a result of this indemnity. Subrogation rights allow third parties who are owed sums by a trustee, who in turn has an indemnity, to proceed direct against the trust fund 'in place of the trustee'. This prevents hardship for the trustee, and reduces the need for separate legal actions. Rights of lien allow the claims of the trustee to an indemnity to be prioritised over those of any third party (assuming the third party is not already a secured creditor) or beneficiary.

instruments, and in accordance with the duties described in Chapter 4.[337] In practice, however, it will be difficult for a trustee to show no personal fault in these circumstances, unless made vicariously liable for the tort of another, e.g. as described at paragraphs A146 to A154 above.

6.102 The indemnity will cover any legal costs which the trustees incur in bringing or defending proceedings in relation to the trust, provided the case does not relate to their own misconduct. The indemnity will not cover acts which were outside the terms of the governing instruments, e.g. unauthorised use of funds. However, where the trustee has acted reasonably and honestly, the protection of section 61 of the Trustee Act 1925, described above, can be invoked to prevent a liability arising in the first place.

6.103 Committee members in unincorporated associations should include an indemnity provision in their governing instruments in order to enjoy equivalent protection to trustees, although it may be available as a matter of general law as a concomitant of the fiduciary duties owed by committee members to the association. There is very little case law on the subject and the precise position is unclear.[338] The scope of the acts covered by the indemnity will be those of the trustee described above, save that acts outside the rules of the association will not be covered, and no relief from the court equivalent to section 61 is available.

6.104 The major weakness of indemnities for non-corporate trustees is that their effectiveness depends upon the indemnifier having funds to recompense the appointee for the liability. Therefore, to the extent that any liability is greater than the assets of the non-corporate PSO, the appointee still has to find the resources personally to meet the liability. This is why the indemnity is of no use if a PSO is insolvent.

6.105 It is for this reason that an exclusion clause in contracts with third parties (discussed above), limiting potential liability to the assets of the trust PSO, is attractive to trustees and committee members in unincorporated associations, although not to third parties themselves.

General availability: corporate structures

6.106 Indemnities are of less importance for appointees in corporate structures, unless the PSO is unable to purchase insurance for its appointees, for which see further below. In general indemnities are not available for classes of appointee (as they are in non-corporate structures), but they may be used on a case by case basis.

6.107 Statutory and chartered corporations do not usually have any express indemnity conferred by statute, and nor do industrial and provident societies. However, appointees to NHS trusts enjoy an indemnity by virtue of section 265 of the Public Health Act 1875.[339] This covers any expenses which they may incur in defending proceedings against them – the presumption being that the immunity will operate to render such claim ineffective. If the immunity does not operate, the indemnity on costs will also fall away.

6.108 In the case of companies, section 310 of the Companies Act 1985 prevents indemnities being offered for any acts by directors which are "negligent, in default, in breach of duty, or in breach of trust". However, more limited indemnities may be offered to cover any costs

---

337 See for example *Benet v Wyndham* (1862) 4 De GF&J 259, where a trustee was held liable for the negligent acts of woodcutters employed upon trust land when they injured a passer-by. However the damages were allowed to be repaid to the trustee, from the trust funds.

338 See J F Keeler *Contractual actions for damages against unincorporated bodies* (1971) 34 MLR 615, which remains one of the most detailed discussions of the subject. It is clear, however, that the indemnity is from the funds of the association, and not from fellow members, unless there is an express term to the contrary: *Wise v Perpetual Trustee Co Ltd* [1903] AC 139.

339 See paragraphs 6.36 ff above for details of this section, in relation to statutory immunity.

incurred by the director in successfully defending proceedings relating to their directorship.[340] Equally, insurance may be purchased to cover personal liability for these wrongful acts by a director.[341] The statutory relief in section 727 of the Companies Act 1985, described above, could also be invoked where claims relate to duties to the PSO. However, insurance will provide wider coverage than the discretion of statutory relief, since the former can cover potential third party claims, while the latter is limited in this respect.[342]

6.109 It is always open to a PSO to provide indemnities to appointees (other than company directors) on a case by case basis. Provided there is power in the governing instruments for an indemnity to be offered there is no reason at law why PSOs should not offer indemnities individually to appointees. Without such express provision, however, the offer of an indemnity would be in breach of the duty not to profit from appointment discussed under Duty 3 in Chapter 4 Section A.

Nominee appointees

6.110 While PSOs themselves are one source of indemnities, some appointees may be able to benefit from indemnities from other locations, regardless of whether the PSO has a corporate or non-corporate structure. Any appointee nominated to serve on a responsible body by a third party is, in theory, capable of receiving an indemnity from that third party, to protect them from the consequences of a personal liability.[343]

This is an attractive source of protection, since the funds for the indemnity would not be those of the PSO, but those of the nominator, with whom the appointee is likely to have a link by employment or public office.

6.111 Provided the terms of the third party's constitution allow it to offer such indemnities, there is no reason why a PSO should not allow an appointee with such indemnities onto its responsible body.

6.112 However, indemnities offered to one particular type of nominee appointee, nominees from local authorities, have recently received judicial attention which has thrown into doubt the legality of indemnities for this class of appointee. The two cases which are at the centre of the concern are *Burgoine & Cooke v Waltham Forest LBC*[344] and *Sutton LBC v Morgan Grenfell*.[345]

6.113 The background to these cases, and an analysis of the judgments, is set out in Appendix E. The difficulty which arises from the judgments is that interpretations of their effect differ.

6.114 Some commentators believe their effect is to make it impossible to offer indemnities to local authority officers or councillors, except where there is a specific statutory power in relation to that particular act.[346] However, others (including the author of this study) would not draw such a wide conclusion from the facts of these particular cases, particularly where council officers are concerned.[347]

---

[340] Directors (as with other appointees in corporate structures) do not need the wider indemnity offered to trustees in relation to the costs of legal proceedings generally, since it will be the corporate body which is sued (and made liable to costs) rather than the individual appointees. Only in cases involving some question about the personal conduct of the director will the indemnity become of relevance. This analysis assumes there is no joint liability (see Appendix C).

[341] S.310 (3) *ibid.*

[342] See paragraph 6.19 above.

[343] This will be the case no matter what the legal structure of the PSO.

[344] The Times 7 November 1996; but reference to the transcript is necessary to understand the full reasoning in the case (CH 1996 No B5222 24 October 1996).

[345] The Times ibid.

[346] See the comments of T Child and J Libovitch in *Indemnities spell double trouble* Local Government Chronicle CIPFA Supplement June 1997 p38; and *Covering your Backs* LGC Law and Administration 27 March 1997 p11.

[347] See for example the analysis by Christopher Baker, Solicitor's Journal 21 March 1997, p257.

6.115 As noted in Appendix E, it is difficult to draw absolute conclusions on the law in the absence of further cases testing the issues. However, until that time is reached, it is important that a consistent line is taken on the interpretation of local authority powers in this respect. The Audit Commission has not issued any technical guidance on the matter, and while it could not seek to dictate to a District Auditor his or her duties in this respect (since the Commission has no jurisdiction in this sense over individual auditors), issuing guidance in a form that sought to apply uniform principles would undoubtedly assist local authorities. The involvement of the Department of the Environment, Transport and the Regions, and representative local authority associations, should also be considered.

PSOs which cannot insure

6.116 The third and final aspect of indemnities which needs to be discussed is the role they can play where personal liability insurance cannot be purchased from a PSO's funds. As shown in Table 3 above, NDPBs and NHS trusts are not able to purchase insurance to cover appointees from personal liability due to rules of government accounting. In order to provide some equivalent protection to their appointees, the Treasury allows PSOs to offer a standard form of indemnity to these individuals.[348] However, there is debate over whether this protection is equivalent to the protection that would have been afforded to such appointees by insurance, as described earlier in this section.

6.117 NDPBs with corporate structures and NHS trusts are unlikely to have personal contractual liabilities or tortious liabilities given the separate legal personality of the PSO except where these are the result of personal acts (although non-corporate NDPBs will have this potential liability).[349] Instead, the indemnity will operate for liabilities which may arise through an appointee's failure to exercise their fiduciary or governance duties properly. The scope of the Treasury indemnity covers appointees where they have acted "honestly, reasonably and in good faith and without negligence in exercise or purported exercise" of their functions.[350] If an appointee to an NDPB meets this test, they will not have to meet any personal civil liability out of their personal resources. The terms of the indemnity would therefore cover *ultra vires* acts by appointees, provided their behaviour complies with the test set out.

6.118 Concern has been expressed that by limiting the indemnity to acts which are both 'reasonable' and 'without negligence', the terms of the indemnity are more limited than would otherwise be available under a commercial insurance policy. Indeed it is questionable what acts of an appointee giving rise to personal liability would be caught by this formula. Unlike insurance policies, which give a broad definition of the 'wrongful acts' covered by the policy and then specify certain behaviour which is not covered,[351] the indemnity provides a broad definition of the characteristics which the appointee must display in order to benefit from the indemnity. This 'person specification' in the indemnity makes it difficult to identify the potential liability which is to be covered since the terms used are notoriously difficult to define at law.

6.119 To give an example, the breach of warranty of authority claim that can arise where an appointee acts without proper authority can lead to liability where the appointee has acted honestly, and in good faith. However, it is difficult to envisage how the appointee will have been acting both

---

[348] Described as a 'Treasury indemnity', the source of funds will actually be the PSO – the sanction of the Treasury for the indemnity ensures that such expenditure is legitimate.

[349] And see Appendix C on the issue of joint liability for corporate acts.

[350] Dear Accounting Officer Letter 3/96 and *Guidance on Codes of Practice for Board Members of Public Bodies* (January 1997) Cabinet Office (OPS) paragraph 27.

[351] See paragraph 6.83 ff above.

reasonably[352] and without negligence (in the sense of lacking care), so as to create a liability in this way. There is likely to be some form of mistake or misunderstanding behind most types of personal liability, and the Treasury indemnity leaves it open to question whether any such error on the part of an appointee will deprive an appointee of this protection.

6.120 Moreover, deciding whether a liability has involved negligence on the part of an appointee is not always easy. While some types of civil liability are clearly recognised as requiring a degree of negligence (e.g. liability for causing personal injury to another person), other cases are not as clear-cut (e.g. liability for wrongful trading).

6.121 Accordingly, interpreting the true protection conferred by the Treasury indemnity is difficult, and comparisons with protection offered by insurance policies suggests that the two are not offering equivalent reassurance.

6.122 A separate concern is how claims are made under the indemnity and where the resources will come from. This should be a less serious problem, since it would require the Treasury to renege on the terms of the Dear Accounting Officer letter for the indemnity not to be honoured. However, the first source of funds for the indemnity will be those of the PSO, and not a separate pool of money provided by the Treasury for the purpose.

Conclusions

6.123 Indemnities are a valuable source of protection for appointees, although they have their limitations for appointees in non-corporate structures when insolvency occurs. Unresolved questions remain about the extent to which indemnities can lawfully be offered to local authority nominee appointees, and about the degree of protection indemnities offer to appointees in NHS trusts and NDPBs when compared to insurance.

6.124 Indemnities will only offer reassurance to appointees if they know they will be able to rely upon them if a personal liability occurs, and they have acted honestly and in good faith. Therefore the legal basis for offering indemnities must be clearly established in all cases, and the scope of behaviour protected must be clearly understood.

---

[352] Presumably according to the standards of a reasonable neutral person, and not the standards of the appointee themselves.

PSOs: information and assumptions

This appendix highlights key facts about the PSOs studied and explains certain assumptions made about them in order to facilitate comparison in the study. It does not provide a full legal analysis of each type of PSO. It should be read in conjunction with Chapter 3: The Legal Structures Explained.

NHS trusts

1 NHS trusts provide and manage hospitals in the public sector (and associated medical facilities), and may be established by order of the Secretary of State for Health under section 5 of the National Health Service and Community Care Act 1990. They are statutory corporations, and can only exist in this one form. They are not trusts in the legal sense of the word.[1] NHS trusts are a class of non-departmental public body, but for the purpose of the study, have been treated as a separate type of PSO.

2 NHS trusts have **boards of directors** as their responsible body, of whom some members will be salaried 'executive' directors with a paid position in the relevant hospital, while others will be 'non-executive' directors from outside. The study is concerned with the non-executive directors (NEDs) of NHS trusts. NEDs are appointed in accordance with regulations made by the Secretary of State for Health (and in some cases the appointment itself is made by the Secretary of

State).[2] NEDs presently receive remuneration of £5,000 per annum.[3]

3 The functions and powers of each trust are set out in the National Health Service and Community Care Act 1990.[4] Public funding is received by trusts from health authorities and GP fundholders. The Department of Health and the NHS Executive have oversight of trusts' activities, but the Board of Directors has responsibility on a day-to-day basis.

4 NHS trusts can have separate charitable funds of which the statutory corporation itself will be a true trustee. These funds, unless of a *de minimis* amount, will be registered with the Charity Commission. The study does not consider the position of such charitable funds, but is only concerned with the general position of non-executive directors of the NHS trust itself.

5 Individual trusts, NHS umbrella organisations and the NHS Executive provided guidance for directors on their role and responsibilities.[5]

Grant maintained schools

6 First introduced in 1988, grant maintained schools (GM schools) are completely independent of their local authority. Existing schools may elect to become grant maintained having followed the procedure laid down by statute.[6] These schools are exempt charities.[7]

---

[1] For a discussion of the status and qualities of the NHS trust, see R Bartleet *When is a "Trust" not a Trust?: the National Health Service Trust* [1996] 60 Conv May/Jun.

[2] See the NHS Trusts (Membership and Procedure) Regulations 1990 (SI 1990/2024) as amended.

[3] The Commissioner for Public Appointments monitors appointments made to trusts by the Secretary of State for Health. See paragraph 42 below.

[4] Schedule 2 and see SI 1990/2024 *ibid* regarding board procedures.

[5] For example, guidance in the form of Corporate Governance Manuals and Executive Letters are issued to NHS trusts.

[6] See Education Act 1996 Part III: new schools may also choose grant maintained status.

[7] Charities Act 1993 Schedule 2.

7 The responsible body of a GM school is incorporated as a **statutory corporation**,[8] and all of the appointees (known as governors) will be the members of the corporation. The governing body owns the school property, employs the staff and is responsible for the school and its operation. GM schools are funded, and therefore regulated by the Funding Agency for Schools[9] (itself an NDPB). The study does not consider the regulation of educational standards etc, e.g. by OFSTED.

8 Detailed rules surrounding the appointment of governors are set out for all GM schools in the school's governing instruments. The basic principle is that governors are elected by different constituencies, e.g. staff and parents. The powers of the governing body are set out in legislation,[10] and every school will have instruments and articles of government regulating the conduct of the school and the responsibilities of governors.[11] In addition, the Funding Agency for Schools requires a financial memorandum with each school from which some duties and responsibilities are derived.

9 Governors are not permitted to receive any remuneration, other than travel and subsistence expenses.[12]

10 Guidance for governors is provided by the Department for Education and Employment, the Funding Agency for Schools, and umbrella organisations such as the Grant Maintained Schools Centre.[13]

11 In July 1997, the Government published a White Paper *Excellence in Schools*,[14] which proposed changes to the school system, to create community, foundation and aided schools. At the time of writing the new status of GM schools is unclear. However it appears likely that they will continue to own school property and employ staff, but their budget may be delegated from the local authority. For the purposes of the study, no account has been taken of the White Paper's proposals.

TECs

12 Training and enterprise councils (TECs) are responsible for promoting and providing vocational education and training for the employed and the unemployed, and for encouraging the development of industry and enterprise for the benefit of the local community. In theory, they are not limited to one specific legal structure, although in practice they are all, with one exception, **companies limited by guarantee**.[15] Accordingly the study assumes they take this structure.

13 The governing instruments for TECs are not prescribed by any regulator or government department. Therefore, as a company, each TEC will have individual memoranda and articles of association which define the powers and duties of the responsible body. However, TECs' work is based upon (and therefore regulated by) a licence and funding contract between the TEC and the Departments for Education and Employment and of Trade and Industry. This licence requires TECs to operate within prescribed guidelines and standards.

---

[8]   Education Act 1996 s.195.

[9]   The funding of GM schools in Wales is the responsibility of the Welsh Office.

[10] Presently Education Act 1996 s.231, although the history of grant maintained schools is such that other legislation (now repealed) may have provided the original basis for the school's powers.

[11] The precise method by which these governing instruments are created depends upon the method of creation of the school: those formed under the Education Reform Act 1988 were provided with models which required approval, while standard instruments and articles of government apply to schools which become grant maintained under the Education Acts 1993 or 1996 (by means of regulation (SI 1993/3102 as amended) and Schedules 22 and 23 of the 1996 Act). All such instruments have common terms.

[12] See, for example, Education Act 1996 s.218 (4) Sch 22 para 15 setting down the requirement for GM schools incorporated under this Act.

[13] For example, the DfEE publishes *School Governors: A Guide to the Law - grant maintained schools* (1994 edition).

[14] CM 3681.

[15] The one exception being Hampshire TEC which is a company limited by shares.

14 Appointments to the **Board of Directors** of a TEC are made by existing members of the TEC, but the criteria for eligibility for the position of director are set by the two above-mentioned government departments. Some directors may also be employees of the TEC (i.e. executive directors). As with NHS trusts, the study is only concerned with non-executive directors.

15 The TEC National Council (an umbrella organisation for TECs) provides guidance on the role and responsibilities of TEC board members.[16]

16 It is a condition of the government licence and funding contract that TEC directors receive no remuneration from any public funds provided by the Government. This will be contained in the governing instruments of each TEC.

Local authority maintained schools

17 Local authority maintained schools are hybrid organisations since they have a degree of autonomy which renders them legally separate from day-to-day control by the local authority, without giving them the degree of independence afforded to grant maintained schools.

18 The responsible bodies of all maintained schools are established as **statutory corporations**.[17] However, there are three different types of maintained school: county (which approximately 75% of pupils in the maintained sector attend); voluntary, which is further divided into controlled, aided and special agreement schools; and special schools. Approximately 20% of pupils in the maintained sector attend voluntary schools, with the remaining 5% attending special schools.

19 The study has taken the county school as the basic model, because in terms of the personal liability of governors, many of the differences between county and voluntary schools go to the character of the school, rather than the legal position of the responsible body. However, the governing body of voluntary schools can have greater responsibility for owning property and employing staff (particularly voluntary aided schools), and in terms of liability to third parties, appointees may be in a similar position to governors of grant maintained schools.[18]

20 The method of appointment of governors for maintained schools will vary according to the type of school. The basic principle is that governors are elected or nominated by different constituencies, including parents and teachers. The powers and functions of the governing body are set out in primary legislation, while the governing instruments for each school are made by order of the local authority, and will be based upon legal requirements set by the Department for Education and Employment, in both primary legislation and by regulation.[19]

21 The study assumes that 'local management in schools' (LMS) is in operation, under which the budget and the management responsibility for the school is delegated to the governing body by the local authority.[20] This permits the governing body greater autonomy, and it is now the case that all maintained schools have LMS, except in cases where it has been suspended.[21]

22 School governors are not permitted to receive remuneration, other than approved travel and subsistence expenses.[22]

---

[16] For example, the TEC National Council publishes an Induction Pack for new directors, and guidance on standards of conduct for directors.

[17] Education Act 1996 s.88 and Schs 7 and 8.

[18] It should also be noted that some voluntary schools will have trust arrangements in connection with their property or funding, e.g. by virtue of particular religious origins. Appointees in these circumstances may have separate responsibilities by reason of these arrangements.

[19] See Education Act 1996 Pt II Chp IV, in particular s.76, Schs 7 and 8 and the Education (School Government) Regulations 1989 (SI 1989/1503) as amended.

[20] See Education Act 1996 Part II Chp V and Schs 11 and 12, and the associated regulations.

[21] There are no known cases of suspension.

[22] Education Act 1996 s. 116(7). Similar rules apply for schools without LMS.

23 The Department for Education and Employment publishes guidance for school governors on their role and responsibilities.[23]

Further education colleges

24 Most colleges providing further education are established as **statutory corporations** under the Further and Higher Education Act 1992,[24] becoming independent of local authority control in the process. However, further education colleges can also exist as trusts, companies limited by guarantee, and in one case, an unincorporated association. Collectively, these other structures are known as 'designated institutions' under the legislation. The study assumes that further education colleges have a statutory corporation structure. FE colleges are exempt charities.[25]

25 The responsible body of a further education college is usually called the **Board of Governors**, with each individual governor being a member of the corporation.

26 Detailed rules for appointing governors are set out in the instrument and articles of government for each college.[26] The basic principle is that governors are elected or nominated by different constituencies, including staff and students. The powers and functions of each college are set out in the primary legislation.[27]

27 Governors are not permitted to receive any remuneration, other than expenses.[28]

28 Funding for further education colleges is provided by the Further Education Funding Councils for England and for Wales, and these bodies (which are themselves NDPBs) exercise some regulatory control over colleges. The Councils publish guidance for college governors on their role and responsibilities.[29]

Universities

29 Following the 1992 education reforms, two types of higher education provider need to be distinguished: the 'old' universities, established for the most part as **chartered corporations**, and the 'new' universities, established mostly as **statutory corporations** under the Education Reform Act 1988, thereby removing them from local authority control.[30] Accordingly, the study refers to these two types of university as 'pre-1992' and 'post-1992' universities respectively. There are examples of universities with a different structure, e.g. corporations at common law,[31] companies limited by guarantee[32] or statutory corporations.[33] The study focuses on the two main types, and both are exempt charities.

30 The responsible body of a pre-1992 university will usually be called the Council, although other

---

[23] For example see the DfEE publication *School Governors: A Guide to the Law (County and Controlled schools)* June 1997.

[24] S.15.

[25] Charities Act 1993 Schedule 2.

[26] Further and Higher Education Act 1992 ss.20, 21 & Sch 4 and the Education (Government of Further Education Corporations) Former Further Education Colleges Regulations 1992 (SI 1992/1963) as amended.

[27] Further and Higher Education Act 1992 ss.18 and 19.

[28] SI 1992/1963 *ibid* paragraph 10.

[29] For example see *Guide for College Governors* FEFC May 1994.

[30] Previously these institutions were polytechnics operated under the aegis of local authorities. The Education Reform Act 1988 originally effected the change to higher education corporations, and amendments made by the Further and Higher Education Act 1992 extended the powers of such institutions to award degrees and use the title 'university'.

[31] E.g. the Universities of Oxford and Cambridge, although the colleges themselves may be chartered corporations.

[32] E.g. the London School of Economics (as part of the University of London).

[33] The Universities of London, Durham and Newcastle all have statutes governing their legal status, which marks them out from the majority of pre-1992 universities.

names are also used.[34] For post-1992 universities the responsible body is known as the **Board of Governors**.

31 The appointment of members of the responsible body in pre-1992 universities will be determined by the governing instruments. Generally, members will include staff and student representatives, members of the Senate, and external members appointed by the Council itself. In post-1992 universities, the governors are nominated by different constituencies, e.g. the local authority, staff and students, as well as independent members. The Secretary of State for Education has powers as regards the initial constitution of the governing body, but thereafter it falls to the Board itself.[35]

32 The governing instruments of a pre-1992 university will be the founding charter, while for a post-1992 university the governing instruments will be made by order of the Privy Council, in accordance with the terms of the Education Reform Act 1988 (as amended).[36]

33 Funds for all universities are provided by the Higher Education Funding Councils for England and for Wales. These impose financial and regulatory requirements on universities, and also publish guidance for appointees.[37]

34 Appointees in post-1992 universities may not receive remuneration save for legitimate expenses.[38] In pre-1992 universities the governing instruments may authorise remuneration or expenses, although this is not believed to be common practice.

Registered social landlords

35 A housing association is a "non-profit-making body that has to do with housing" (e.g. providing, constructing, improving or managing housing).[39] A housing association can exist in a number of legal forms. For the purposes of the study the structure of the **industrial and provident society** has been chosen, although associations can also exist as companies or trusts. The study does not distinguish co-operatives from other types of housing association.

36 In order to receive public funds from central government (as opposed to being purely private concerns), housing associations must be registered with the Housing Corporation, which means, following the reforms of the Housing Act 1996, that they must qualify as 'social landlords' within the meaning of section 2.[40] Therefore, the term 'registered social landlord' is used in the study to mean housing associations which meet the above criteria.

37 The responsible body of a registered social landlord (RSL) is usually known as its **Executive Committee**, with each appointee being a member of the RSL's corporate body (although the total membership may well be wider than this). The means of appointment are not regulated by any particular statutory rules, and the governing instruments will determine how each appointment is to be made.

38 The governing instruments of an RSL, usually termed its 'rules', will be developed by each individual association, but will need to comply

---

34 The Council is distinct from the university body usually known as the Senate which has responsibility for academic affairs. In addition, many institutions have a Court which sits above the Council, but which is not in day-to-day charge of the affairs of the university. See the discussion in Farrington *Law of Higher Education* (1994) chapter 4 (Butterworths).

35 See Education Reform Act 1988 Schs 7, 7A.

36 S.124A, Schs 7 and 7A.

37 For example see the guide issued by the Committee of University Chairmen in association with the HEFC *Guide for Members of Governing Bodies of Universities and Colleges in England and Wales* (June 1995).

38 See Education Reform Act 1988 Sch 7 para 11, and Sch 7A para 9.

39 Alder & Handy *Housing Association Law* (2nd edition) Sweet & Maxwell p3.

40 The 1996 Act creates a broader definition of organisations entitled to register with the Corporation than the now repealed provisions of the Housing Associations Act 1985.

with the requirements of the Registrar for Friendly Societies and the Housing Corporation. Model terms are provided.

39 The Housing Corporation has both a funding and a regulatory role, and provides guidance for committee members on their role and responsibilities, as does the umbrella organisation, the National Federation of Housing Associations.[41] Committee members may only receive very limited remuneration in addition to expenses.[42]

40 Registered social landlords which are industrial and provident societies are exempt charities.[43]

NDPBs

41 The NDPBs studied are executive NDPBs, rather than advisory NDPBs or tribunals, and examples of the work they perform are outlined in Chapter 3. Generally, such NDPBs have a corporate structure and can exist as **companies limited by guarantee, or statutory or chartered corporations**. However, it is possible for NDPBs to exist with the non-corporate structure of a **trust**. NDPBs may also be exempt charities, such as the National Museums and Galleries,[44] but NDPBs do not enjoy Crown immunity.[45]

42 The membership of the responsible body of an NDPB, often known as its **Board,** will be appointed by the Secretary of State within whose department the NDPB falls. The Office of the Commissioner for Public Appointments monitors the appointment process for NDPBs, in accordance with published Codes and Guidance on such appointments.

43 In general appointees will receive no remuneration for their services for a PSO, other than expenses, although the governing instruments may permit it.

44 The nature of the governing instruments will depend upon the NDPB's legal structure. Guidance for appointees will often be published by the host department or the NDPB itself, and generic guidance on the position of NDPBs is issued by the Cabinet Office.[46]

Registered charities

45 Registered charities may take one of three legal structures: **a trust, an unincorporated association or a company limited by guarantee** (referred to as 'charitable companies' in the study). It is the choice of the original founders of the charity which structure they adopt. Where the study refers to the rules relating to registered charities it means they apply to any of these structures, unless the contrary is stated.

46 The terms used for the responsible body and appointees for charities will vary according to the particular structure: they may be **trustees, committee members or directors**. Although the Charities Act 1993 and the Charity Commission adopt the term 'trustee' to cover all appointees to registered charities, the study does not adopt the same terminology. Appointees are referred to as 'trustees' only when they serve a trust PSO.

---

[41] See, for example, the publications of the Corporation including the *Guide to Regulation of RSLs*, and those of the NFHA. The NFHA publication *Housing Associations and their committees: A guide to the legal framework* (Taussig), is still a useful source of advice although published before the 1996 Housing Act (separate NFHA guidance is produced on the Act).

[42] Housing Act 1996 Schedule 1, and see Appendix B.

[43] Charities Act 1993 Schedule 2. Note, however, that registered social landlords need not have charitable status to be registered with the Housing Corporation, following the 1996 Housing Act reforms.

[44] See Schedule 2 Charities Act 1993.

[45] The exceptions being the Health and Safety Executive and ACAS; and see footnote 25 on page 16.

[46] See, for example, *Guidance on Codes of Best Practice for Board Members of Public Bodies* Cabinet Office (OPS) January 1997.

47 There is a general presumption that appointees to registered charities will not receive remuneration. However if (and only if) the governing instruments of a PSO permit it appointees may receive a salary, although the approval of the Charity Commission is required to add such a clause where the founder has not provided for it.[47] In practice most appointees to registered charities remain unpaid, save for expenses.

48 The terms of the governing instruments will need to conform with Charity Commission requirements before an organisation can register with the Commission. Model terms for all three types of structure are available for newly established charities, and guidance on the role of the appointee is available from the Charity Commission.[48]

---

[47] See Appendix B.

[48] See Commission Leaflet CC1 for full details of their publications.

Appendix B

Appointees' remuneration

PSO	Appointees' remuneration
NHS trust non-executive directors	£5,000 per annum (maximum)[1]
GM school governors	Travel and subsistence only[2]
LA school governors	Travel and subsistence only[3]
TEC non-executive directors	Legitimate expenses only[4]
Appointees to registered charities	No prohibition: presumption against[5]
Registered social landlord committee members	Expenses and limited payment only[6]
Pre-1992 university council members	Presumption against[7]
Post-1992 university board members	Travel and subsistence only[8]
FE college governors	Travel and subsistence only[9]
NDPB board members	No absolute rule[10]

[1]   The National Health Service and Community Care Act 1990 permits payment to appointees (Schedule 2 para 9) – this is the current annual limit.

[2]   The governing instruments will specify the requirement: see, for example, Education Act 1996 s.218(4), Sch 22 para 15.

[3]   The governing instruments will specify the requirement: for schools with LMS (see Appendix A) see Education Act 1996 s.116(7).

[4]   This is a requirement of the DfEE/DTI Licence and will be contained in the memorandum and articles of each TEC.

[5]   There is no bar to trustees, directors or committee members receiving remuneration if the terms of the governing instruments allow it; however, it is not common practice for such a term to be included. The Charity Commission will require evidence that a remuneration clause is necessary and reasonable in the interests of the charity before agreeing to the inclusion of such a term or a one-off payment: see *Decisions of the Charity Commissioners* volume 2 (1994).

[6]   The Housing Act 1996 contains new rules on the benefits which committee members may now receive: see Schedule 1. While remuneration is now permitted, the current maximum determined by the Housing Corporation is £50 per year: HC Circular R5-37/96 and Version 4 Corporation Guidance on payments and benefits.

[7]   The governing instruments may permit remuneration or expenses, but it is not believed to be common practice.

[8]   The governing instruments will specify the requirement: see Education Reform Act 1988 as amended, Sch 7 para 11; Sch 7A para 9.

[9]   The governing instruments will specify the requirement: see the Education (Government of Further Education Corporations) (Former Further Education Colleges) Regulations 1992 SI 1992/1963, paragraph 10.

[10] If the governing instruments (frequently a statute) permit remuneration, board members may accept it. The practice of government departments establishing NDPBs varies, but service without any remuneration is common practice for PSOs.

Appendix C

Corporate acts and personal liability

Introduction

1   The discussion in Chapter 4 has highlighted the importance of a corporate PSO's separate legal personality when it comes to appointees' personal liability. One of the reasons a corporate structure is so beneficial to appointees is that it allows the PSO to commit corporate acts.[1] If such corporate acts turn out to be unlawful and harm a third party, the PSO itself can generally be made liable for the act.[2]

2   However, as described in Chapter 4 Section B, the protection afforded by corporate status is not all-embracing. In particular, where an individual appointee is involved in an event which harms a third party, difficult questions of shared or apportioned liability can arise. Much will depend upon the degree to which the act can be said to be a personal act.

3   The question addressed in this appendix is whether an appointee can be jointly liable with the PSO for a PSO's corporate acts which cause loss or injury to other people or organisations.[3] This appendix is not relevant to non-corporate PSOs and their appointees.

Corporate acts

4   Since a PSO relies upon its appointees to control its affairs it follows that appointees will be responsible for taking the decisions which lead to corporate acts being undertaken. However, because such acts are attributable to the PSO, the generally held view of the law (and that stated by most legal textbook writers) is that appointees are not capable of being jointly liable for such acts.[4]

5   This is in contrast to the position of employees and agents of a PSO whose wrongful acts (e.g. torts) will give rise to potential liability for the PSO (as principal or agent) and the concerned individual, provided the act was undertaken within the scope of their authority or employment.[5] It will be the choice of any wronged third party whether they sue the individual, the PSO or both.[6]

6   The rationale for this distinction between appointees and employees or agents is that since corporate PSOs have deliberately adopted a separate legal personality, the appointees who stand behind that personality should not be responsible for corporate acts, even wrongful ones, unless they are clearly personal ones.[7] Conversely, the acts of agents or employees may be connected with the PSO's activities but they are not concerned with directing the PSO's affairs: they are not 'corporate acts'.

---

[1]   Another reason is the availability of limited liability status.

[2]   The different types of liability that can arise from such acts, for example by failing to fulfil the duties imposed by social regulation, are discussed in Chapter 4, Sections B and C.

[3]   The types of wrongful act under consideration here are breaches of common law duties, e.g. torts, rather than statutory duties, since, as explained in Chapter 4 Section B, statutory duties can expressly impose joint liability on an appointee and the PSO in any event.

[4]   See, for example, *Clerk & Lindsell on Torts* (17th ed 1995) para 4-47.

[5]   See Chapter 4 Section B for definitions of these terms.

[6]   The decision may be influenced by the availability of insurance and which of the two has the 'deeper pockets'. Note also that the employee may be liable to indemnify the employer, so that the employer can recover any damages from its employee (to the extent of the employee's solvency): *Lister v Romford Ice and Cold Storage Co* [1957] AC 555.

[7]   See paragraph 8(a) below on the position of appointees as agents.

7 If legally correct, this proposition confers a valuable protection on appointees. However, it is open to some doubt since the legal cases cited to support the proposition may not provide a conclusive foundation.

Joint liability

8 The generally held view of the law on joint liability can be set out in three stages:

(a) Where the corporate acts of appointees are *intra vires* and in good faith they are acts for which the corporate body (the PSO) alone will be liable, even if they subsequently prove to be tortious.[8] The case cited to support this is *Mill v Hawker*.[9] The agreed exception to this is where an appointee is specifically made an agent for some purpose (i.e. outside the normal office of appointee) in which case the rules concerning the joint liability of principal and agent, set out above, apply.[10]

(b) The case of *Mill v Hawker* is then used as the basis for asserting that where corporate acts are *ultra vires*, the corporate body would not be liable, and any loss or damage would fall to the appointees personally. However, a later case contradicts this proposition, and supports the view that *ultra vires* acts too are corporate acts for which the corporate body alone will be liable, provided the appointees act in good faith: *Campbell v Paddington Corporation* [1911] 1 KB 869.[11] Therefore there is some legal uncertainty about the position of appointees if the corporate acts are *ultra vires*.[12]

(c) If the appointees do not act in good faith (i.e. the conduct was wilful and malicious) then appointees become personally liable for the act, even if carried out in a corporate capacity: *R v Watson* (1788) 2 TR 199. In this situation the act is the personal act of the appointee.

9 These propositions need to be examined, however, to see what support the cases cited provide for them.

Mill v Hawker

10 The case of *Mill v Hawker* concerned the acts of members of a highway board who had ordered a surveyor to remove an obstruction placed upon a disputed highway, and who with the surveyor were sued for trespass. The court held, by a majority, that the orders of the members were unlawful, because they were outside their powers, and that therefore the members were personally liable. The dissenting judgment held that the orders were corporate acts which were *intra vires* and therefore the corporate body should have been sued (and that even if the acts were *ultra vires*, they were still corporate acts for which the corporate body would be liable since they had been expressly authorised).

11 In giving the majority judgment Cleasby B concentrated on the effect of the acts being *ultra vires* on the potential liability of the members. He said:

> "We were referred to many authorities to show that in respect of corporate acts the individual members of the corporation

---

8 *Clerk & Lindsell on Torts op cit; Salmond & Heuston Law of Torts* (21st ed 1996) pp 407–408.

9 (1874) LR 9 Ex 309; (1875) LR 10 Ex 92.

10 Therefore, to the extent that advice is given that appointees are constitutionally incapable of being jointly liable, this is wrong – they can be made agents on the particular facts of any case.

11 Note that the discussion of *ultra vires* acts in Chapter 4 Duty 4 considered acts such as entering contracts, where the act could be void depending on the legal structure of the PSO (companies and chartered corporations being subject to different rules to statutory corporations and industrial and provident societies). Here, while the act might be *ultra vires* it will have caused harm to a third party and so is distinguished from acts such as entering contracts.

12 See the detailed discussion in *Clerk & Lindsell on Torts op cit*, para 4-45.

cannot be sued. . . . And it is clear that this is so when the corporate acts are such as the corporate body is qualified to perform, and the resolutions and acts of the members are only introductory to the corporate body acting in the matter."[13]

12   This has been relied upon, together with the dissenting judgment of Kelly CB (insofar as it states the law, rather than reaching a conclusion on the facts) to support the proposition that there can be no joint liability for corporate acts: the act will either be that of the corporate body or that of the individual appointees.

Contrary view

13   However, criticism of the above view of the law stems from uncertainty about the extent to which *Mill v Hawker* provides a firm foundation for it. As indicated above, the majority judgment concluded that individuals cannot be sued for corporate acts where the acts were *intra vires* and where the resolutions and acts of the members were only introductory to the corporate body acting in the matter. As stated above, the *intra vires* point has been doubted subsequently. On this basis *Mill v Hawker* may stand for no more than the principle that if appointees' involvement is no more than preparatory to a corporate act, they will not be liable. There are no express words in the judgment which support the general conclusion that joint liability is impossible for appointee and corporate PSO.

14   Therefore, the distinction between personal acts and corporate acts may be more blurred, so that the liabilities of PSO and appointee are not mutually exclusive, and an action could be maintained against appointee and PSO for an apparently corporate act.

Conclusions

15   It is not possible to say which of these two views on corporate acts is correct.

16   The first view (that there is no joint liability) certainly has the force of frequent repetition, and is supported by the logic of corporate status discussed at the beginning of the appendix. Furthermore, drawing an analogy between appointee and PSO and employee and employer to the effect that both situations should lead to joint liability ignores the fact that the employee must indemnify the employer in such circumstances; ultimately the liability will rest with the employee (but a third party is given the ability to sue either). It is not clear whether appointees could owe or be owed a similar indemnity if joint liability was established for corporate acts.

17   The second view, based on the judgment in *Mill v Hawker* itself, has sufficient weight to raise doubts over the definitive advice on the question of joint liability.

Practical consequences

18   While this debate over joint liability is one of detailed legal analysis, and may seem academic, it has produced practical consequences for some PSOs. Appointees to NHS trusts in Wales have been advised that the law which applies to their corporate acts is that of the 'contrary view' outlined above: there could be joint liability.[14] Thus, appointees in these organisations have been informed that there is the potential for joint liability for corporate acts. It is also understood that a similar view is taken by the NHS Executive in England.[15]

---

[13]   P317 of judgment (see footnote 9 above).

[14]   See the advice published by the Welsh Office for directors of NHS trusts in Wales on 21 May 1997 (WHC(97)14).

[15]   An Executive Letter to this effect is expected shortly.

19   The consequence of this is that the indemnity
      provided by the Treasury (see Chapter 6 above)
      may need to be more widely drafted to explicitly
      refer to the possibility of liability for joint acts
      which are nonetheless corporate based.

20   This view of the law appears to be in contrast
      to that taken by other government departments,
      where joint liability is not raised as an issue.
      For example, the guidance produced by the
      Department for Education and Employment for
      school governors in grant maintained and local
      authority maintained schools makes no reference
      to the concept of joint liability, relying instead on
      the separate corporate status of the governing
      body, except where acts are not performed in
      good faith.

21   Neither of these positions can be judged the
      better guidance. In an increasingly litigious society
      it is not surprising that attention has been paid to
      how effective the protection of corporate status is
      for PSOs. At present, however, there is no uniform
      guidance for appointees who serve in PSOs
      of similar legal structure, but who fall under
      the auspices of different regulators and
      government departments.

Appendix D

Statutory and chartered corporations and the rights of creditors

Introduction

1   As explained in Chapters 3 and 5, appointees to statutory and chartered corporations benefit from limited liability as far as the debts of the PSO are concerned. It is the legal personality of the PSO to which creditors must look for satisfaction, and appointees are not liable except to the extent that the governing instruments state otherwise.[1]

2   However, Chapter 5 showed how limited liability has been undermined for two types of corporate structure, the company and the industrial and provident society, following creation of the remedy of wrongful trading, under the Insolvency Act 1986.

3   This appendix considers what happens to the outstanding liabilities of statutory and chartered corporations in the event of dissolution, and whether their appointees can be made liable under these same provisions.

Dissolution regime

4   A short introduction to the methods of dissolution of statutory and chartered corporations was given in Chapter 5.

Statutory corporations

5   As explained, for statutory corporations it is usual for the Secretary of State to take control of the dissolution powers. A summary of the different provisions for the PSOs studied is set out in Table 5 at the end of this appendix.

6   The points common to all these PSOs are that:

   (a) dissolution requires the approval or order of the Secretary of State;
   (b) a complete regime is provided, allowing for the allocation of assets, rights and liabilities of the dissolved PSO to third parties; and
   (c) insolvency is not singled out for any special treatment in the dissolution process.

7   In all cases a discretion is given to the Secretary of State (and funding councils or local authorities in certain circumstances) to determine whether to approve dissolution, and if so on what terms. This means that there is no absolute certainty that a decision to dissolve will be made. However, the discretion is amenable to judicial review, and in an insolvency situation a refusal to dissolve the PSO (or properly allocate its liabilities) would probably be capable of challenge.[2]

8   In the (unlikely) event that dissolution occurred, but liabilities remained which were unallocated to a third party, the limited liability rules pertaining to the corporation and its appointees should operate to protect the appointees. In these circumstances the liabilities would go unmet.

Chartered corporations

9   The regime for dissolving chartered corporations is not set out as clearly as for statutory corporations, at least as far as insolvency is concerned. In the absence of provisions in the charter itself detailing how matters are to be dealt with on insolvency, it will be left to a court to determine matters (on an application to dissolve the corporation) or for the appropriate Act of Parliament revoking the charter to apportion liabilities.

---

[1]   No examples of which have been found in the PSO context.

[2]   The one exception to this is NHS trusts where there is now no discretion. If a trust ceases to exist the Secretary of State must secure the transfer of its residual liabilities to ensure they are dealt with: National Health Service (Residual Liabilities) Act 1996.

10 As with statutory corporations, in the event that liabilities remained undischarged upon dissolution, the limited liability rules pertaining to the corporation and its appointees should operate to protect the appointees. In these circumstances the liabilities would go unmet.

Application of Insolvency Act 1986

11 Given the various means of dissolution outlined above, the question arises whether the wrongful trading remedy provided by the Insolvency Act 1986 (the Insolvency Act) for creditors of companies and industrial and provident societies could be made available to creditors of statutory and chartered corporations. The analysis that follows indicates that it would not.

12 The Insolvency Act applies to companies registered under the Companies Acts and to industrial and provident societies (as described in Chapter 5), but it also applies to 'unregistered companies'.[3] While neither statutory nor chartered corporations fall within the first two definitions, consideration needs to be given to whether they could constitute unregistered companies, and therefore be liable to be wound up under that Act.

13 The definition of an unregistered company for these purposes is a wide one, and includes any association and any company "not already registered under legislation relating to companies".[4] At first glance it is not readily discernible how a statutory or chartered corporation is to be dealt with under this definition. While formed for purposes other than profit, many statutory corporations operate in a commercial world, supplying goods and services to the public. Does this make them unregistered companies? In the case of chartered companies, the courts have held that they are unregistered companies subject to similar (earlier) winding-up provisions.[5]

14 However, case law considering earlier similar enactments has held that the term applies only to trading companies (with a place of business), to be distinguished, for example, from a literary institution or a members' club.[6] Thus a chartered company carrying on business for profit can be distinguished from a chartered corporation established to provide education.

15 In the case of statutory corporations, reasoning in one case is cited as authority that these are not to be treated as unregistered companies, on the basis that statutory corporations do not possess the qualities of a business, e.g. there are no profits to be distributed, and all funds come (ultimately) from the tax-payer.[7] Support for the view that a court would continue to treat a modern statutory corporation as distinct from a 'trading company'[8] is provided by the case of *In re International Tin Council*.[9] Here the Court of Appeal held that when construing the word 'association' (for the purposes of applying insolvency law) it could not include an organisation which Parliament could not reasonably have intended to be subject to

---

[3] Ss.220–229.

[4] S.220 (1) *ibid*. Certain other exceptions, irrelevant to PSOs, are also specified.

[5] See *Halsbury's Laws of England* vol 9 para 1397 and *Re English Scottish and Australian Chartered Bank* [1893] 3 Ch 385.

[6] See *Re Bristol Athenaeum* (1889) 43 Ch D 236, and the commentary in *Halsbury's Laws of England* vol 7(3) 1996 reissue, paras 2899–2907.

[7] See *Tamlin v Hannaford* [1949] 2 All ER 327 at 328 D–H, and *Halsbury's Laws of England* vol 7(3) para 2902.

[8] The corporation in the *Tamlin* case was akin to an executive NDPB, with greater ministerial controls over its affairs than some of the recently created education and health statutory corporations.

[9] Court of Appeal judgment only: [1989] 1 Ch 309.

[10] The case concerned the application of earlier statutory provisions relating to winding up unregistered companies to an organisation established by treaty. Nourse LJ cited with approval the authority of *In re St James Club* (1852) 2 De GM&G 383 in support of the court's conclusions.

the winding-up jurisdiction.[10] By analogy, a court is likely to follow the same line of reasoning in construing 'company', were it ever argued that a statutory corporation should come within the Insolvency Act's ambit.[11]

corporations, it seems highly improbable that a court would hold Parliament to have intended statutory (or chartered corporations) to be subject to insolvency law as unregistered companies. On this basis, the wrongful trading remedy should not be available against appointees to these PSOs.

16 Since a complete regime has been provided by Parliament for dissolution of statutory

Table 5 – Statutory corporations and dissolution procedures

PSO	Statutory provisions for dissolution	PSO able to request dissolution?[1]	Consultation requirements[2]	Property, rights and liabilities transferable?
Grant maintained schools	Ss.267–279 Education Act 1996 (consolidating and repealing ss. 111–116 Education Act 1993). Dissolution made by order of Secretary of State.[3]	The school or the funding authority may propose *discontinuance* of the school (to be approved by the Secretary of State in certain circumstances).	Yes	Funding authorities may make grants to the governing body for the purpose of discharging any relevant liability (s. 276 EA 1996). Surplus assets remaining pass to the Secretary of State (s. 279 *ibid*).
Local authority maintained schools	S.88 and Sch 7 paras 6–10 Education Act 1996 (consolidating and repealing Sch 13 paras 8–12 Education Act 1993). Dissolution automatically follows discontinuance of school (para 6(1)).	Discontinuance will result where the local authority ceases to maintain the school (following approval by Secretary of State in certain circumstances)[4] ss.167–175 Education Act 1996.	Yes	All property, rights and liabilities vest in local education authority upon dissolution.[5]

[11] The definition of 'unregistered company' in the Companies Act 1985 is narrower than that in the Insolvency Act 1996 (and specifically excludes "any body incorporated by or registered under any public general Act of Parliament and any body not formed for the purpose of carrying on a business which has for its object the acquisition of gain" s.718(2). However, for the purposes of determining whether a body can be wound up under insolvency law, it is the Insolvency Act definition which applies.

PSO	Statutory provisions for dissolution	PSO able to request dissolution?[1]	Consultation requirements[2]	Property, rights and liabilities transferable?
Further education colleges (FE corporations)	S.27 Further & Higher Education Act 1992. Dissolution by statutory instrument made by Secretary of State.	The funding councils may propose it – but the statute is silent on the right of the corporation itself to petition.	Yes	Secretary of State may transfer to another educational body (with recipient's consent) or a funding council.
Post-1992 universities (higher education corporations)	S.128 Education Reform Act 1988. Dissolution by statutory instrument made by Secretary of State.	The funding councils may propose it – but the statute is silent on the right of the corporation itself to petition.	Yes	Secretary of State may transfer to another educational body (with recipient's consent) or a funding council.
NHS trusts	Sch 2 para 29 NHS & Community Care Act 1990. Dissolution by Statutory Instrument made by Secretary of State.	Yes	Yes (unless required as matter of urgency)	Property/liabilities may be transferred to (a) the Secretary of State; (b) a health authority; (c) another NHS trust.

[1]   For some PSOs there is a distinction between the PSO ceasing to carry out activities (discontinuance) and the formal step of winding it up (dissolution), e.g. for grant maintained schools. For others, the steps are not so separated, e.g. further education colleges.

[2]   Consultation required if PSO has not requested dissolution.

[3]   But not by statutory instrument: s.568 (1) (2) Education Act 1996.

[4]   If a voluntary school, the governors may propose discontinuance.

[5]   Subject to any property which is held upon trust (e.g. in a voluntary school).

Nominee appointees and local authority indemnities

Introduction

1   Local authorities frequently nominate officers or councillors to serve on the responsible bodies of PSOs (as well as other organisations working for the benefit of the community). For example, local authorities nominate governors to maintained schools, and registered charities and social registered landlords often have a local authority representative on their responsible bodies.

2   In addition to any protection afforded to such nominee appointees by virtue of their service for the PSO, these appointees can, in theory, take the benefit of a contractual indemnity from the local authority itself. However, in order to be valid, the proper powers must be available to the local authority to grant the indemnity. There are three potential sources of such power:

   (a)   A specific statutory provision giving a power of indemnity or guarantee for the particular purpose, e.g. section 22 of the Housing Act 1996;[1]
   (b)   Section 112 of the Local Government Act 1972, which allows councils to employ staff to discharge the council's functions on reasonable terms and conditions; and
   (c)   Section 111 of the Local Government Act 1972, which provides implied powers for the council to do "any thing ... which is calculated to facilitate or is conducive or incidental to the discharge of any of their functions".

3   However, a number of recent judicial decisions have considered the extent to which councils can use the three methods described above to give indemnities and guarantees to their own employees or to third parties. The result of these cases has been to cast doubt on methods (b) and (c) as the basis for granting indemnities.

4   The cases concerned are described below, together with an analysis of the effect of each case.

5   As will be shown, while the cases do raise concerns, particularly for council members (as opposed to employees), the belief expressed by some commentators that method (a) above provides the only power for granting an indemnity, in any circumstances, is probably going too far on the basis of the case law as it presently stands.[2]

Background

6   In order to understand the case law, two situations need to be distinguished:

   (a)   The case where the council nominates an appointee to a PSO, and *has* a statutory power to carry out the function of the PSO concerned (e.g. to provide housing or education facilities); and
   (b)   The case where the council nominates an appointee, but *does not have* the statutory power to perform the function to be carried out by the PSO.

---

[1]   This provision relates to guarantees, but there is no difference in the result achieved between a guarantee and an indemnity. The latter is more usual when promising to reimburse someone for a personal liability they have suffered.

[2]   See, for example, articles by T Child and J Libovitch: *Indemnities spell double trouble* Local Government Chronicle CIPFA Supplement June 1997 p38; and *Covering your Backs* LGC Law and Administration 27 March 1997 p11, and discussed further below.

7 Since local authorities are creatures of statute (a particular type of statutory corporation), they only have those powers which they are expressly or impliedly given by statute. They cannot act as a natural person would.

8 The power relating to a council's ability to undertake a particular function is different from the power to actually give the indemnity, but, as set out below, the absence of the power to do the particular thing may affect the powers described at paragraph 2 (a) to (c) above to give the indemnity.

9 Turning to the particular cases:

Burgoine & Cooke v Waltham Forest London Borough Council – The Times 7 November 1996[3]

Facts

10 The *Burgoine* case concerned the nomination of two Council officers to the board of directors of a joint venture company to provide leisure services in the form of a 'water park' for the borough.[4] The project failed, and the company went into liquidation. An action directly against the local authority to enforce a guarantee, issued by it to a bank involved in the venture, failed when it was held that the acts of the local authority in setting up the joint venture were *ultra vires*.[5] An action for 'wrongful trading' (amongst other things) was then brought by the liquidator against the Council officers, as directors.[6]

11 The officers had the benefit of a contractual indemnity from the local authority, which they sought to enforce to recover the costs of defending the liquidator's action against them, together with any award of compensation against them that might result therefrom.[7]

12 Following the intervention of the District Auditor, Neuberger J was asked to determine the question of whether or not the indemnity given by the local authority was within its powers, and if so, whether it protected the officers from any liability which might arise in the wrongful trading proceedings.

13 It was agreed (following the previous proceedings) that the Council had been acting beyond its powers when it set up the joint venture company, and therefore had no power to nominate the officers to serve on its behalf.

Judgment

14 The judge held that the officers could not rely upon the indemnity granted to them by the Council. This was because the particular words used in the indemnity required the officers to be acting "in or about the pursuit of their duties on behalf of the Council" and " within the scope of their authority" in order to be protected. The judge held that as the acts of the Council were *ultra vires*, the acts of the officers could not be said to fall within this particular definition as a matter of construction: they could never be acting "on behalf of the Council" because the authority had no power to appoint them so to do.[8]

15 Thus, without needing to look at the Council's powers to grant the indemnity, the judge held that this particular indemnity did not cover the acts of the officers, and therefore could not be relied upon.

---

[3] The following analysis is based upon the full transcript (CH 1996 No B5222 24 October 1996).

[4] This was not, therefore, strictly speaking a PSO, but this does not affect the relevance of the decision on the question of indemnities.

[5] Decision of Michael Barnes QC sitting as Deputy Judge of the High Court: *NWS 6 Ltd v Waltham Forest LBC* unreported 17 November 1992.

[6] Section 214 Insolvency Act 1986 and see Chapter 5 above.

[7] The joint venture company itself could not indemnify the officers (s.310 Companies Act 1985), but it could have taken out insurance to protect them.

[8] The Judge also held that no reliance could be placed on section 265 of the Public Health Act 1875 since the offence of wrongful trading was one based on negligence, and the immunity and indemnity conferred by this provision did not cover negligence – see Chapter 6 above for discussion of this question.

16 However, having heard arguments on the matter, the judge went on to consider what the position *would have been* if the actual terms of the indemnity had covered the acts of the officers.[9] This meant considering the terms of section 112 of the Local Government Act 1972 (LGA), under which the indemnity had been granted.

17 Neuberger J did not accept arguments that section 112 could never be used to grant an indemnity where the Council had acted *ultra vires* in nominating the officers to the outside organisation. It would, he held, be a matter to be decided on the particular facts. However, he believed that where a council purported to give an officer a task which they both wrongly, but bona fide, believed fell within the ambit of the officer's lawful employment, then section 112 (2) did not preclude a valid contractual indemnity for that task.

18 Equally, the judge rejected an argument that the acts of the officers as directors were automatically outside the scope of their duties for the local authority because they were serving in another capacity. It would be a question of fact in every case, but there was nothing mutually exclusive about representing the council on the one hand (as official) and serving as directors of the company on the other.

Analysis

19 The *Burgoine* case is concerned with the interpretation of a particular contractual indemnity. However, it raises the question of whether section 112 provides a valid power for granting an indemnity, where the local authority has no capacity to nominate the officer. The *Burgoine* judgment does not hold that section 112

cannot be used in these circumstances (assuming the words of the indemnity itself are wide enough to cover acts in these circumstances). Whether or not Neuberger J's conclusions on the point would be followed is open to question,[10] but without a further court case to determine the point conclusively, the *Burgoine* case should not be extended too far in its application to indemnities generally.

20 Equally, the *Burgoine* case had nothing to say on indemnities granted where the local authority does have the power to nominate the officer. Yet some commentators have suggested that section 112 cannot be used for indemnities in these circumstances either, as a result of the cases discussed below.[11]

21 These cases do not involve consideration of section 112 LGA and indemnities for officers, but, rather, indemnities and guarantees offered to third parties, using the implied powers offered by section 111 LGA.

Sutton London Borough Council v Morgan Grenfell & Co Ltd – The Times 7 November 1996

Facts

22 The *Sutton* case concerned an arrangement between the Council and an unregistered housing association to provide temporary accommodation for the homeless. Under the arrangement, the Council gave a guarantee to a bank lending money on the project, and indemnified the association against any losses it might suffer. The association went into liquidation, and the bank and the liquidator of the association sought to enforce the guarantee and indemnity.

---

9 Such wording could have been that the indemnity would cover acts "purportedly in pursuit of the council's functions provided they were undertaken in the honest and reasonable belief that the council could legitimately pursue such functions'.

10 A counter argument to Neuberger J's reasoning is that the requirement that employees are to be engaged to carry out the proper discharge of the council's functions (112 (1)) means that *ultra vires* acts are not within the scope of employment, and that an indemnity offered under section 112(2) must only relate to the "proper discharge of functions" so interpreted. This argument was put to Neuberger J, but rejected – see pp27–29 transcript.

11 See Child and Libovitch *op cit*, where it is acknowledged that the *Burgoine* case did not rule on this point, but where it is suggested that in any circumstances only express statutory powers (paragraph 2 (a) above) provide a lawful basis for issuing an indemnity.

Judgment

23   The Court of Appeal held that the Council did not have the power to give the guarantee since the specific statutory provisions dealing with the Council's grant of guarantees in these circumstances restricted it to dealings with registered housing associations.[12] By implication, the indemnity was also prohibited. Therefore, both were void. Reliance could not be placed on the powers in section 111 of the LGA, since these could not be used as additional powers where there were already detailed statutory provisions concerning the particular statutory function being undertaken.[13]

24   In reaching this conclusion the court relied upon earlier Court of Appeal judgments in *Credit Suisse v Allerdale Borough Council* and *Credit Suisse v Waltham Forest LBC*,[14] in which the application of section 111 LGA was considered in detail. Here, in two separate judgments the Court held, *inter alia*, that there needed to be express statutory provisions conferring power on a local authority to give an indemnity, and that section 111 could not be relied upon where Parliament had already established detailed rules for controlling the financial affairs of local authorities.

Analysis

25   All three of the above-mentioned cases concerned indemnities or guarantees offered to third parties (not members or employees of the council). The consequence which arises from the decisions is that it is now difficult for a local authority to rely upon section 111 LGA as a basis for granting an indemnity. This is because any function exercised by a local authority will be prescribed by statute, and unless that particular provision gives a power to indemnify, section 111 cannot be used to add in powers to indemnify which are not already provided.

26   In relation to PSOs, this affects council members who are nominated to responsible bodies (since section 112 does not apply to them). In these circumstances, district auditors may well take the view that an indemnity relying on section 111 powers for a council member is an improper use of the section 111 power and, therefore, is ineffective.[15]

27   However, it is not clear that the judgments concerning section 111 can be used as a basis for holding that section 112 is also an ineffective means of granting indemnities to employees. In the *Sutton*, *Allerdale* and *Waltham Forest* cases the court was concerned with indemnities granted to third parties, as commercial transactions (albeit for beneficial public purposes). The indemnity granted to an employee (under section 112) is arguably a different type of transaction, connected to the employment of the officer, rather than the external dealings of the local authority. No conclusive view can be reached on this question without a further court ruling. In the absence of such a case it must be open to authorities to apply a less restrictive interpretation to section 112 than is now being applied to section 111.

---

12   Ss.58 and 69 Housing Associations Act 1985 (now repealed and replaced by the Housing Act 1996).

13   Per Gibson LJ.

14   [1996] 3 WLR at 894 and 943 respectively.

15   It seems probable that the council could purchase insurance under its section 111 powers to cover council members for any personal liability sustained while acting as a nominee appointee for the PSO, at least in cases where the council had the statutory power to undertake the particular function. However, district auditors will treat such expenditure on a case by case basis. Such insurance could also be purchased under section 112(2) for council officers. The premiums for such policies would, of course, be much smaller than the potential liability under an indemnity and, therefore, may be seen as a more economic use of public funds (assuming the risks being insured against are properly identified).

Table of cases

Case

Aberdeen Ry Co v Blaikie Bros (1854) 1 Macq 461.
p32 f104

Albion Steel & Wire Co v Martin [1875] 1 Ch D 580.
p34 f112

Alsop, Whitaker v Bamford: Re [1914] 1 Ch 1. p68 f281

Armitage v Nurse The Times 31 March 1997. p71 f300;
p78 para 6.88

Att-Gen v Cocke [1985] Ch 414. p66 f274

Att-Gen v De Winton [1906] 2 Ch 106. p32 f105

Att-Gen v Ross [1985] 3 All ER 334. p44 f171

Att-Gen v Leicester Corporation [1943] 1 Ch 86. p17 f30

Baker v Jones [1954] 1 WLR 806. p44 f168

Bamford v Bamford [1970] Ch 212. p73 f309

Baroness Wenlock v River Dee Co (1883) 36 Ch 675.
p43 f162

Bartleet v Barclays Bank Trust Co [1980] Ch 515. p29 f77

BBC v Johns [1964] 1 All ER 923. p17 f31

Benet v Wyndham (1862) 4 De GF&J 259. p81 f337

Bishopsgate Investment v Maxwell [1993] BCC 120.
p35 f121

Boardman v Phipps [1967] 2 AC 46. p35 f126

Boulting v Association of Cinematograph [1963] 2 QB 606.
p34 f118

Bradley Egg Farms v Clifford [1943] 2 All ER 378. p25 f60

Bray v Ford [1896] AC 44. p33 f109

Brazilian Rubber Plantation and Estates Ltd [1911] 1 Ch 425.
p27 f66

Bristol Athenaeum: Re (1889) 43 Ch D 236. p60 f249;
p98 f6

British South Africa Co v De Beers Ltd [1910] 1 Ch 354.
p43 f162

Bullard v Croydon Health Group Management Committee
[1953] 1 QBD 511. p70 para 6.37

Burgoine & Cooke v Waltham Forest LBC The Times
7 November 1996. p70 f296; p82 para 6.112;
p102 para 10 ff

C Evans Ltd v Spritebrand Ltd [1985] 1 WLR 317.
p50 f196

Campbell v Paddington Corporation [1911] 1 KB 869.
p94 para 8(b)

City Equitable Fire Insurance: Re [1925] Ch 407. p27 f64

Claridges Patent Asphalte: Re [1921] 1 Ch 543. p68 f282

Collen v Wright (1857) 7 E & B 301, affd (1857) 8
E & B 647. p40 f148

County Palatine Loan Co: Re (1874) 9 Ch App 691.
p38 f136

Cowan v Scargill [1985] Ch 270. p28 f75

Credit Suisse v Allerdale Borough Council [1996] 3 WLR 894.
p43 f160; p104 para 24

Credit Suisse v Waltham Forest LBC [1996] 3 WLR 943.
p104 para 24

Customs & Excise Commrs v Hedon Alpha Ltd [1981]
QB 818. p67 f278

D'Jan of London: Re [1993] BCC 646. p28 f68

Dominion Students' Hall Trust: Re [1947] Ch 183.
p29 f78, f79

Dorchester Finance Co Ltd v Stebbing [1989] BCLC 498.
p27 f64

English Scottish and Australian Chartered Bank: Re [1893]
3 Ch 385. p98 f5

George Whitechurch Ltd v Cavanagh [1902] AC 117.
p41 f155

Turner, Barker v Ivimey: Re [1897] 1 Ch 536.
p67 f279; p68 f283

Vernon's Will Trusts: Re [1972] 1 Ch 300. p29 f82

Vickery: Re [1931] 1 Ch 572. p46 f181

Waterman's Will Trusts v Sutton: Re [1952] 2 All ER 1054.
p29 f77

Whiteley: Re [1910] 1 Ch 600. p37 f132

Whitworth Art Gallery Trusts: Re [1958] 1 All ER 176.
p60 f251

Wise v Perpetual Trustee Co Ltd [1903] AC 139.
p20 f45; p81 f338

Worrall v Harford (1802) 8 Ves 4. p80 f335

Yonge v Toynbee [1910] 1 KB 215. p40 f148

Table of legislation

Selected bibliography

Legal texts

Alder and Handy *Housing Association Law* (2nd ed) Sweet & Maxwell

Brazier et al *Clerk & Lindsell on Torts* (1995 17th ed) Sweet & Maxwell

Cairns *Charities: Law and Practice* (3rd ed 1997) Sweet & Maxwell

Davies *Gower's Principles of Modern Company Law* (6th ed 1997) Sweet & Maxwell

Farrington *Law of Higher Education* (1994) Butterworths

Guest et al *Chitty on Contracts* (27th ed 1994) Sweet & Maxwell

Hayton *Underhill and Hayton on the Law of Trusts and Trustees* (15th ed 1995) Butterworths

Heuston and Buckley *Salmond & Heuston on the Law of Torts* (21st ed 1996) Sweet & Maxwell

McGillivray on Insurance Law (9th ed 1997) Sweet & Maxwell

Merkin *Colinvaux's Law of Insurance* (7th ed 1997) Sweet & Maxwell

Oakley *Parker & Mellows on the Modern Law of Trusts* (6th ed 1994) Sweet & Maxwell

Palmer's Company Law (Looseleaf) Sweet & Maxwell

Pennington *Company Law* (7th ed 1995) Butterworths

Percy and Walton *Charlesworth and Percy on Negligence* (9th ed 1997) Sweet & Maxwell

Picarda *The Law and Practice Relating to Charities* (2nd ed 1995) Butterworths

Rabinowicz et al *Education Law and Practice* (1996) FT Law and Tax

Reynolds *Bowstead & Reynolds on Agency* (16th ed 1996) Sweet & Maxwell

Taussig *Housing Associations and their Committees: A Guide to the legal framework* (1992) National Federation of Housing Associations

Wade and Forsyth *Administrative Law* (7th ed 1994) Clarendon Press

Warburton *Unincorporated Associations* (2nd ed 1992) Sweet & Maxwell

Warburton *Tudor on Charities* (8th ed 1995) Sweet & Maxwell

Reports and guidance

Charity Commission Publications – Annual Reports, Decisions and Guides

Governance of public bodies – a progress report Cm 3557 (February 1997) The Stationery Office

Government Accounting The Stationery Office (1989 as amended)

Guidance on codes of practice for board members of public bodies Cabinet Office (January 1997)

Guide for college governors Further Education Funding Council (May 1994)

Guide for members of the governing bodies of universities and colleges in England and Wales CUC and the Higher Education Funding Council (June 1995)

Guide to the regulation of registered social landlords Housing Corporation (January 1997)

Local Public Spending Bodies Second Report of the Committee on Standards in Public Life (May 1996) – Cm 3270 HMSO

Meeting the challenge of change: voluntary action into the 21st century – The report of the Commission on the Future of the Voluntary Sector, NCVO Publications (1996)

NDPBs – A Guide for Departments Cabinet Office/OPS (1992 as amended)

Public Bodies 1997 The Stationery Office (December 1997)

Responsibilities of Senior Management Consultation Paper 109 Securities and Investment Board (July 1997)

Rights of creditors against trustees and trust funds – A Consultation Paper Trust Law Committee (April 1997)

School Governors – A guide to the law (grant maintained schools – 1994); (county and controlled schools – June 1997) Department for Education and Employment

Standards of conduct in local government in England Scotland and Wales Third Report of the Committee on Standards in Public Life (July 1997) – Cm 3702 The Stationery Office

Trustees powers and duties Law Commission Consultation Paper 146 (April 1997)

Printed in the United Kingdom for The Stationery Office
J0050468, C20, 6/98, 5673.